Engaging Ethically in a Strange New World

Australian College of Theology Monograph Series

SERIES EDITOR GRAEME R. CHATFIELD

The ACT Monograph Series, generously supported by the Board of Directors of the Australian College of Theology, provides a forum for publishing quality research theses and studies by its graduates and affiliated college staff in the broad fields of Biblical Studies, Christian Thought and History, and Practical Theology with Wipf and Stock Publishers of Eugene, Oregon. The ACT selects the best of its doctoral and research masters theses as well as monographs that offer the academic community, scholars, church leaders and the wider community uniquely Australian and New Zealand perspectives on significant research topics and topics of current debate. The ACT also provides opportunity for contributors beyond its graduates and affiliated college staff to publish monographs which support the mission and values of the ACT.

Rev Dr Graeme Chatfield
Series Editor and Associate Dean

Engaging Ethically in a Strange New World

A View from Down Under

Edited by
MICHAEL BRÄUTIGAM
and GILLIAN ASQUITH

WIPF & STOCK · Eugene, Oregon

ENGAGING ETHICALLY IN A STRANGE NEW WORLD
A View from Down Under

Australian College of Theology Monograph Series

Copyright © 2019 Wipf and Stock Publishers. All rights reserved. Except for brief quotations in critical publications or reviews, no part of this book may be reproduced in any manner without prior written permission from the publisher. Write: Permissions, Wipf and Stock Publishers, 199 W. 8th Ave., Suite 3, Eugene, OR 97401.

Wipf & Stock
An Imprint of Wipf and Stock Publishers
199 W. 8th Ave., Suite 3
Eugene, OR 97401

www.wipfandstock.com

PAPERBACK ISBN: 978-1-5326-8803-4
HARDCOVER ISBN: 978-1-5326-8804-1
EBOOK ISBN: 978-1-5326-8805-8

Scripture quotations marked HCSB are from the Holman Christian Standard Bible®. Copyright © 1999, 2000, 2002, 2003 by Holman Bible Publishers. Used by permission. Holman Christian Standard Bible®, Holman CSB®, and HCSB® are federally registered trademarks of Holman Bible Publishers.

Scripture quotations marked NRSV are from the New Revised Standard Version Bible. Copyright © 1989 National Council of the Churches of Christ in the United States of America. Used by permission. All rights reserved worldwide.

Scripture quotations marked ESV are from The Holy Bible, English Standard Version® (ESV®). Copyright © 2001 by Crossway, a publishing ministry of Good News Publishers. All rights reserved.

Scripture quotations marked NASB are from the New American Standard Bible®. Copyright © 1960, 1962, 1963, 1968, 1971, 1972, 1973, 1975, 1977 by The Lockman Foundation. Used by permission.

Scripture quotations marked NET are from the New English Translation Bible®. Copyright ©1996–2016 by Biblical Studies Press, L. L. C. All rights reserved.

Scripture quotations marked NIV are from The Holy Bible, New International Version® NIV®. Copyright © 1973, 1978, 1984, 2011 by Biblica, Inc.TM Used by permission. All rights reserved worldwide.

Manufactured in the U.S.A.

Contents

Contributors | vii
Abbreviations | xi
Editorial | xiii

Part 1: Engaging Ethically within Christian Community

1. Ethics in the Old Testament Wisdom Books | 3
   —ANDREW BROWN

2. Deciding about Deciding: Early Christian Communal Decision-Making in Acts | 27
   —STEVE WALTON

3. Jonathan Edwards on Contemplating the Beauty of Christ | 50
   —MICHAEL BRÄUTIGAM

4. Does Talking about Theological Ethics or Moral Theology Vaporize Christian Ethics? | 68
   —MARK W. ELLIOTT

Part 2: Engaging Ethically with Wider Society

5. The Ethics of Jesus: The Paradox of Jesus's Strenuous Demands and Inclusive Lifestyle | 87
   —GREG W. FORBES

6. Islam and Homosexuality | 101
   —BERNIE POWER AND PETER RIDDELL

CONTENTS

7 Living with "Assisted Dying": An Introduction to the Issues and Ethics of Voluntary Euthanasia and Assisted Suicide in Australia | 124
—DENISE COOPER-CLARKE

8 The Virtue of Docility in Global Theological Conversation | 141
—THOMAS KIMBER

Contributors

Michael Bräutigam studied psychology in Germany (University of Trier) and theology in Scotland (University of Edinburgh). He teaches in both disciplines at Melbourne School of Theology. His doctoral dissertation focuses on the Christology of Swiss theologian Adolf Schlatter (1852–1938), published as *Union with Christ: Adolf Schlatter's Relational Christology* (Pickwick, 2015; in German with TVZ, 2017). His current research focuses on the integration of theology and psychology with a particular emphasis on Christian identity.

Andrew Brown lectures in Old Testament and Hebrew at Melbourne School of Theology. Andrew grew up in Australia and completed undergraduate degree studies in both New York State and Tennessee, USA. Following a short stint of Bible college teaching and administrative work, he completed more formal theological college studies. Soon after arrival at Melbourne School of Theology, Andrew completed his PhD, a history of Christian interpretation of the creation week in Genesis 1:1—2:3.

Denise Cooper-Clarke is a graduate of medicine and theology with a PhD in medical ethics (end-of-life decision-making). She is an occasional adjunct lecturer in ethics at Ridley Melbourne, a voluntary researcher with ethos: Evangelical Alliance Centre for Christianity and Society, Moderator for Philosophy and Ethics for the Australian College of Theology, and a member of the Social Responsibilities Committee of the Anglican Diocese of Melbourne. She has particular interests in virtue ethics, professional ethics, and sexual ethics.

CONTRIBUTORS

Mark W. Elliott is Professor of Theology at the University of Glasgow and Professorial Fellow at the University of Toronto (Wycliffe College), having been Professor at St Andrews University. He is from Glasgow, educated at Oxford, Aberdeen, and Cambridge and recipient of a von Humboldt stipendium for research stays at Heidelberg and Munich. He has written on providence both in terms of the history of the idea and of the biblical and theological foundations. He specializes in the history of biblical exegesis and doctrine.

Greg W. Forbes has had close ties with Melbourne School of Theology since he commenced undergraduate studies at the college in 1986. After completing a BTh in 1991, he has since completed an MTh on Revelation 20 and was awarded a PhD from Deakin University for a thesis on the parables in Luke. At Melbourne School of Theology, Greg serves as Senior Lecturer and Department Head of Biblical Studies. Research interests include Synoptic Gospels, General Epistles, and Greek grammar as it relates to exegesis.

Thomas Kimber serves as Dean of Faculty and Senior Lecturer in Missional and Pastoral Theology at Melbourne School of Theology. He has ministered for more than thirty years through teaching, preaching, writing, and mentoring. Tom and his wife, Sue, served as missionaries in Asia for nearly nine years, before returning to the United States, where Tom taught at Biola University. Tom holds both MDiv and PhD degrees from Talbot School of Theology. Tom's area of research interest includes the integration of spiritual formation in missiology and pastoral theology.

Bernie Power is a lecturer in Islamic Studies at the Arthur Jeffery Centre for the Study of Islam, Melbourne School of Theology. He holds degrees in science, arts, and theology. His doctorate, on comparative religion, compares early Islamic and Christian texts, and he has published three books and many articles in this field. With his wife and family he spent over twenty years living and working among Muslims in Asia and the Middle East.

Peter G. Riddell is Vice Principal Academic at Melbourne School of Theology and Professorial Research Associate in History at SOAS University of London. His research focuses on Southeast Asian Islamic history and theological texts, with particular reference to interpretation of the Qur'an. He has published six books, sixteen edited volumes, and over eighty scholarly articles and chapters in refereed journals and books on his fields of research.

CONTRIBUTORS

Steve Walton is Associate Research Fellow and Tutor in New Testament at Trinity College, Bristol, UK. Steve has published a number of books and articles, particularly on the Gospels and Acts, and is presently working on a major commentary on Acts for the Word Biblical Commentary Series. He serves as Secretary of the British New Testament Society, and has been elected as a member of the international Society for New Testament Studies.

Abbreviations

ANH	Artificial nutrition and hydration
BAFCS	The Book of Acts in Its First Century Setting
BECNT	Baker Exegetical Commentary on the New Testament
BibInt	Biblical Interpretation
BZNW	Beihefte zur Zeitschrift für die neutestamentliche Wissenschaft
ESV	English Standard Version
HCSB	Holman Christian Standard Bible
JSJSup	Journal for the Study of Judaism Supplement Series
JSNT	Journal for the Study of the New Testament
JSNTSup	Journal for the Study of the New Testament Supplement Series
LXX	Septuagint
MT	Masoretic Text
NASB	New American Standard Bible
NET	New English Translation
NIV	New International Version
NRSV	New Revised Standard Version
NT	New Testament
OT	Old Testament
PAS	Physician-assisted suicide
PDE	Principle of Double Effect

ABBREVIATIONS

PBUH	Peace be upon him
SNTSMS	Society for New Testament Studies Monograph Series
WBC	Word Biblical Commentary
WJE	Works of Jonathan Edwards
WUNT	Wissenschaftliche Untersuchungen zum Neuen Testament
ZTK	Zeitschrift für Theologie und Kirche

Editorial

CHRISTIANS IN AUSTRALIA ARE facing serious ethical issues. Contentious topics, such as same-sex marriage, the assisted dying bill, gender fluidity, and attempts to censor Jesus-talk in the schoolyard, present serious challenges and require us to think more deeply about how we are to live in a strange new world. The 2018 Paradosis Conference at Melbourne School of Theology offered a platform for theological reflection around these important matters and we are delighted that we are now able to offer in this volume some of the material presented. Our contributors take up the challenge to explore the foundations and practice of Christian ethics and their implications for the church, ministry, mission, the academy, and our own personal contexts. Part one of this volume examines ethical questions of interest within the Christian community, whilst the second part offers a broader perspective as the contributors engage with questions that relate to wider society. In presenting the following chapters, we invite readers to reflect more deeply on living as followers of Jesus in this strange new world of post-Christianity.

Part 1: Engaging with Christian Community

Andrew Brown explores ethics in the Old Testament wisdom books. The relevance of Old Testament wisdom writings has survived the passing centuries rather well, with Proverbs texts being among those that Christian readers today find most approachable. Yet the wisdom of a book like

Proverbs seems very broad compared to the redemptive story of Israel and the church of Christ. Not only is there little direct connection to the gospel of Christ, but many times Old Testament wisdom sayings do not even seem very theological. They can read more like good common sense advice. Andrew deals with the question of how the Christian reader is to interpret the teachings of the Old Testament wisdom books concerning right and wrong conduct in God's world.

According to *Steve Walton*, decision-making today in Western countries is governed by a democratic model, where the majority's will decides what happens. This is true in most Western Protestant churches, where a voting model decides who will be the church's pastor, what the church will give to missions, and so on. The early church's decision-making in Acts is a significant contrast to this approach, and is both strongly communal and dependent on God. Steve shows in his chapter how central the communal life is to earliest Christianity in Acts, and illustrates this with key decisions, including the choice of Matthias (1:15–26) and the Spirit's call of Barnabas and Saul from Antioch (13:1–3). Steve's chapter then takes the gradual inclusion of Gentiles in the believing communities as an extended "case study" for how decisions were made. It closes with reflections on the implications for church decision-making today if the Acts model is taken seriously.

Mark W. Elliott presents an intriguing walk through the theological history of ethics. In his unique *The Making of Moral Theology*, Jack Mahoney argued that, arising in the early modern period, a rules-based approach to Christian ethics took hold, resulting in a particular approach by the Catholic Church's moral theologians that was to the detriment of spirituality and spiritual theology. In Protestant circles, dogmatic theological principles when applied directly to the discipline of ethics, as in the twentieth-century neoorthodox rediscovery of the priority of dogmatics over ethics, occluded spiritual theology as a reflection on spirituality as having a mediating and contextualizing, hence "concretizing" function for moral theology. By considering both earlier and recent attempts to work ethics as theology (Hauerwas and O'Donovan) and in the light of principles of church renewal, Mark makes suggestions both to supplement and to bring out the best of these divergent approaches. Christian ethics, Mark argues, can be theological, spiritual, moral, and concrete.

In my own contribution, I (*Michael Bräutigam*) offer some pastoral reflections on Jonathan Edwards's view of contemplating the beautiful Christ.

Jonathan Edwards had a keen eye for beauty. He saw beauty in creation and discovered here the fingerprints of the beautiful God. This chapter traces the basic thrust of Edwards's reflections on beauty, focusing in particular on the beauty of the Godhead and the believer's participation in God's own beauty. Edwards explores the beautiful interactions of love and harmony in the fellowship of the Trinity and focuses especially on the beauty (or, excellency) of the Son of God. Moving from intra-Trinitarian reflections to theological anthropology, Edwards claims that believers, who are, through the Holy Spirit, equipped with a new sense of the heart, see in Jesus true beauty. What is more, as they contemplate the beautiful Jesus Christ, they are being transformed into his image. Contemplation and moral transformation are thus for Edwards two sides of the same coin.

Part 2: Engaging with Wider Society

Greg W. Forbes investigates the "Paradox of Jesus's Strenuous Commands and Inclusive Lifestyle." Although the ethics of Jesus have occasioned considerable debate in New Testament scholarship, both with respect to their authenticity and interpretation, without doubt Christians today look to Jesus not only as the founder of their faith, but as one to emulate. His teaching is demanding, confronting, and uncompromising. Jesus is also remembered as one regularly associating with those on the margins of society: sinners, prostitutes, and tax collectors. And yet, surprisingly, his demanding teaching does not occur in the context of this association. So, a paradox exists. Those whom we would expect to distance themselves from Jesus given, for instance, his rigorous sexual and financial ethical teaching, gravitate towards him. The guardians of the law and morality, on the other hand, tend to oppose him. This paradox needs explanation, Greg argues, and how we do so has important ramifications for Christian social ethics today.

Bernie Power and *Peter Riddell* offer a fascinating view on Islam's approach to homosexuality. While Western countries have experienced dramatic shifts in attitudes to homosexuality in recent decades, the Muslim world appears on face value to be a bastion of traditional opposition to more liberal attitudes on the gay question. Nevertheless, this topic is much discussed and debated in certain Muslim circles. This chapter considers the textual ingredients drawn on by such Muslims in shaping their views. Particular attention falls upon the Qur'an, Islam's primary sacred text, and the vast body of exegetical literature that has emerged over the centuries.

Bernie and Peter also consider the extent to which the Qur'an and its commentaries provide ingredients for Muslim attitudes and debates about homosexuality in today's world. A historical analysis reveals that, apart from the first 150 years of Islam, the practice of homosexuality was widespread in Islam in many places. Participants included political leaders at the highest levels, for example, caliphs, as well as poets, soldiers, and scholars. In response, the Saudi-inspired Wahhabi movement called for a return to traditional values as represented in the primary texts. Five points along a spectrum illustrate the views held by Muslims today. They range from proscription, including the death penalty, to denunciation, to acquiescence, to private practice, to open advocacy.

Denise Cooper-Clarke deals with the contentious subject of "assisted dying." Now that "assisted dying" has been legalized in Victoria, and may well be in other Australian states and territories, there are important lessons to be learned for Christian communities before such laws come into effect (in Victoria, in 2019). In the public debate, opponents of "assisted dying" relied heavily on consequentialist arguments while proponents argued on the basis of the principles of respect for individual autonomy and of the obligation to relieve suffering, mainly through emotive appeals based on anecdotes of "bad deaths." Arguments on the basis of the principles of the sanctity of human life and of biblical justice were largely missing. Should we rethink our reliance on consequences rather than principles in future discussion on this and other public moral issues? Within Christian communities, an alternative to both principles and consequences, virtue ethics, might be a more fruitful approach. Denise suggests in her contribution that we need to form communities based on an alternative narrative to the culture that enthrones individual choice as the ultimate value that trumps the common good, and that regards all suffering as meaningless and to be avoided at all costs.

Thomas Kimber engages in a global theological conversation from the (neglected) perspective of virtues. The past century has witnessed a dramatic shift in the global center of the church. While the church in the majority world is growing and maturing, the church in the West is in steep decline. Yet, even in the midst of this shift, to what degree is the Western church listening to the voices of the global South and East? Tom explores the importance of educating for virtue, in particular the virtue of docility, and its role in fostering healthy conversation in the church today. The primary mark of docility is a readiness and willingness to be taught. Thomas

Aquinas considers docility to be the foundation of all other virtues and the foundation of our development as rational beings. Michael Barber believes that "one of the key tasks of moral education involves converting the child's originary docility into a lasting virtue." Jonathan Edwards suggests that our growth in virtue is nothing less than our participation in the divine life, which results in a deepening love for God and love for neighbor. In this chapter, Tom seeks to understand virtue from a theological perspective and considers the implications in teaching, pastoral theology, and mission.

We are grateful to Megan Powell du Toit and our series editor, Graeme Chatfield, both of the Australian College of Theology, for their expertise and support. We also wish to acknowledge the pioneering vision of Justin Tan, Vice Principal Academic of Melbourne School of Theology, whose facilitation of the first Paradosis Conference in 2016 was the inspiration for our subsequent conference in 2018. It is our hope that the chapters in this volume will challenge readers in Australia and beyond as a matter of urgency to wrestle biblically and creatively with integrating Christian ethics for everyday life, and equip them to engage their own societies and contexts with the disarming beauty and timeless truths of the Christian faith.

Melbourne, April 2019
Michael Bräutigam and Gillian Asquith

Part I

Engaging Ethically within
Christian Community

I

Ethics in the Old Testament Wisdom Books

Andrew Brown

Everyone in Australia knows the song "Waltzing Matilda." Some, in moments of mild nationalistic madness, have even suggested that it become Australia's national anthem. (Anyone conscious of the typical attitude of our political leaders to fringe benefits would not voluntarily install a song celebrating sheep rustling as the national song.) "Waltzing Matilda" narrates events that take place around a billabong, but not everyone knows what a billabong is. In other countries a billabong may be called an "oxbow lake"; it is a cut off meander beside a river's course, left isolated when a looping river bend is cut through at the base. Wisdom literature can be a kind of billabong where our primary approach to teaching the Bible, especially the Old Testament/Hebrew Bible, is along biblical-theological lines. Since biblical theology favors the tracing out of redemptive history, biblical genres that are historical, such as Samuel through to Kings, or historically embedded, such as torah within the Pentateuchal narrative, or even historically locatable, such as some content from the prophetic books, may seem more important than wisdom and poetic books.

There is great value in a biblical-theological approach to teaching the Bible, but those of us who value the NT principle that "all Scripture is inspired by God and useful for teaching"[1] may feel compelled to return to

---

1. 2 Tim 3:16 (HCSB).

the OT wisdom tradition to retrieve its particular ethical and theological resources. We turn our attention to the canonical wisdom books, Job, Proverbs, and Ecclesiastes,[2] to examine their contribution to biblical teaching on ethics. Given the general lack of interest of these books in much of the historical and covenantal heritage of Israel, we need to find another basis for the theological relevance and ethical authority of these books if they are to form a meaningful part of the Christian biblical corpus. I intend here first to outline the way in which covenant forms the theological basis for ethics in the OT outside the wisdom books, then propose a four-part scheme of the inbuilt "orders" of creation to explicate worldview assumptions that underlie both wisdom and non-wisdom OT books to differing degrees, before exploring the creation underpinnings of ethics in the wisdom books, and finally touching on some of the particularities of these individual books' ethical contributions.

The Covenant Path to Ethics

To establish a contrast with the ethics of wisdom, let us first consider two key theological bases for ethics in the rest of the OT canon outside of the wisdom books. These twin bases find their fundamental grounding in the nature and being of God but yield ethical implications for life via different routes. Both paths presume election; God (Yahweh) has invited, almost compelled, Israel to join him in the bonds of covenant, and her ethical responsibilities issue from this relational status.

The first theological base is grounded in the character or nature of God. We might illustrate this using what is probably the most defining verse of the book of Leviticus: "I am the LORD, who brought you up out of Egypt to be your God; therefore be holy, because I am holy" (Lev 11:45).[3] Clearly the choosing and saving work of Yahweh is a precondition for this call to holiness. While we read of other nations being held accountable for unethical behavior, even where that behavior was not directed against Israel or Judah (Amos 2:1–3; Hab 2:6–17), we do not, to my knowledge, read where the LORD calls them to be holy as he is. This is a covenant-based demand, yet it is not grounded directly in the obligation of God's people

---

2. I am thinking here of the Protestant/Hebrew canon, and thus leave out of consideration the significant apocryphal wisdom books Sirach/Ecclesiasticus and Wisdom of Solomon.

3. All biblical quotes are from NIV 2011 unless indicated otherwise.

to obey their Lord's commands. It is a call to communal conformity to the character of God for the sake of genuine fellowship with him. "Do two walk together unless they have agreed to do so?" (Amos 3:3). How can Israel experience any kind of proximity to a holy God unless she becomes holy?

Admittedly the kind of holiness envisaged in a book like Leviticus is a sacral or ceremonial holiness that appears somewhat alien to a secular, Western reader today. It is for the maintenance of this holiness that someone defiled by contact with a corpse, for instance, must retreat "outside the camp" (Num 5:1–4).[4] Yet there is a powerful ethical model here whose application outlasts the end of a sacral and sacrificial system of worship. It is the ethical imperative for the people of God to become increasingly like God, that the children might increasingly resemble the divine parent. This is the much-discussed and partly implicit ethical norm of *imitatio Dei*, the imitation of God; its rationale is "the life of God models the moral life."[5] It naturally extends beyond sacral purity to moral and ethical life, as is clear in the context of the famous statement of Jesus in the Sermon on the Mount, "Be perfect, therefore, as your heavenly Father is perfect" (Matt 5:48).[6] We can see, too, how the morality obliged by imitation of God might naturally extend well beyond the ethical requirements of just treatment of our fellow humans to issues of private conduct, attitude, motivations, values, and loyalties. Who we are within our hearts and within our homes falls within the parameters of holiness before God.

The second theological base for ethical behavior is found in the mandates of God as the master of the covenant and the covenant people. Exodus 19 famously describes Israel on the threshold of the formalization of the covenant relationship with Yahweh. He issues his challenge to them:

> You yourselves have seen what I did to Egypt, and how I carried you on eagles' wings and brought you to myself. Now if you obey me fully and keep my covenant, then out of all nations you will

---

4. See below on the sacral order.
5. Birch, "Ethics," 342.
6. The rendition of the Gk τέλειος by the English term "perfect" is open to debate; it may make the summons sound more impossible than is really intended. However, a survey of reputable English translations shows a reluctance on translators' parts to choose any alternative to "perfect," e.g., NIV, ESV, NET, HCSB, NASB (1995), NRSV. I would see this as a problem of connotation rather than denotation. In denotation terms, the translation is justifiable, but it gives an impression that probably was not intended either by Jesus or by the OT text that is most likely being alluded to, Deut 18:13, which exhorts Israel to be "blameless" (תָּמִים, *tāmîm*) before her God.

> be my treasured possession. Although the whole earth is mine, you will be for me a kingdom of priests and a holy nation. (Exod 19:4–6a)

With reference to the covenant with Abraham and the patriarchs, the deliverance from Egypt amounts to fidelity to a prior promise and an existing relationship (Gen 15:13–18). Yet with reference to the Sinai covenant, rescue from Egypt in Exod 1–18 represents a grand gesture of goodwill made in advance of the mutual obligations of covenant. Now Yahweh invites Israel to sign on the dotted line, and as she does, she both initiates herself into covenant privileges and commits herself to covenant obligations. Yahweh becomes the true Master, and his will for her conduct becomes mandatory. Notice how the same rare term, "treasured possession" (סְגֻלָּה, *sĕgullâ*), already seen in Exod 19:5, reappears in Deuteronomy's elaborate call to obedience:

> For you are a people holy to the LORD your God. The LORD your God has chosen you out of all the peoples on the face of the earth to be his people, his treasured possession . . . Therefore, take care to follow the commands, decrees and laws I give you today. (Deut 7:6, 11)

Imitation of God is therefore matched by the more concrete idea of obedience to God for the child of the covenant. To enter into such a covenant involves a submission to God's will. Furthermore, there is a clear ethical consequence for the treatment of God's other covenant people. While the torah contains legal protections even for foreign travelers, prisoners of war, and especially foreign-born permanent residents (גֵּרִים, *gērîm*), who in a sense have come partially under Israel's "covenant umbrella" through their residence in the covenant land, covenant privileges are the natural right of the son or daughter of Israel. The offensiveness of the social oppression condemned by the prophets arises from the fact that powerful Israelites were exploiting fellow heirs of those covenant privileges. A clear example from the narrative books would be the desire of Ahab, king of Israel, to take possession of the conveniently located vineyard of Naboth. Ahab is initially offering payment, rather than seeking to seize it by force, but Naboth is entirely within his rights, covenantally speaking, to retain ownership of "the inheritance of my ancestors" (1 Kgs 21:3) given the fundamental inalienability of land within the covenant ideal (Lev 25:23).[7] So

---

7. Wright, *God's People*, 151–53; Wright, *Old Testament Ethics*, 88–92.

the core ethical imperative for a member of the people of God is to permit one's fellow member to enjoy fully all the privileges that come with covenant relationship along with oneself, and that "regardless of their class or stature."[8] The king is not above the covenant's obligations (Deut 17:18–20), nor is the slave beneath its benefits (Deut 5:14).

Thus far are the covenant bases for ethical living: imitation of God and obedience to God. Where, then, does ethical living find its basis in our OT wisdom books, given the low profile of covenant concerns in these books?

Background to Wisdom Teaching about Ethics: The Created Orders

The same twin ethical imperatives of devotion to God and just treatment of one's fellows emerge prominently in our wisdom books, anchored once again in the nature and activity of God, but instead of that anchorage being God's holy nature and his saving and covenanting activity, it here becomes God's creative activity and corresponding sovereignty.

To understand fully how ethical living stems from God's creative activity according to the wisdom books, we may need to expand our concept of what creation entails. As modern, Western readers, we tend to think of creation as God's production of the physical cosmos and of humanity as representing the most noteworthy element of that creation, thanks to the unique human potential for relationship with God. However, readers of the OT wisdom books face the implicit assumption not just of a physical order, but also of moral and social orders, and to these I would add a sacral or spiritual order, intended to cover the abovementioned sacral perspective of Leviticus.[9] The idea here is that there are systems of the world's operation beyond the physical sphere that so occupies the Western mind, and that all of them reflect the being of God and/or constitute the creative construction of God.[10] We should not think that these ideas are *limited* to the wisdom literature; it arguably extends throughout the OT. Yet awareness of them is

---

8. The wording comes from Seow, "Job," 96. It applies as well to a covenant framework.

9. Perdue, "Cosmology," 458–59; Rad, *Wisdom in Israel*, 74–96, 144–76, 302; Van-Drunen, "Wisdom," 153–56; Brown, *Wisdom's Wonder*, 17–18. This is just a sample of the relevant literature.

10. I would note that just how prominent the idea of these orders is in the wisdom literature is open to some debate.

necessary to explain how human ethical conduct relates to the creative role of God according to the wisdom books.

Let us touch on each of these "orders" in turn.

The Physical Order

God's creation of the physical world is clearly celebrated in the wisdom literature. We read in Prov 3:19–20, "By wisdom the Lord laid the earth's foundations, by understanding he set the heavens in place; by his knowledge the watery depths were divided, and the clouds let drop the dew." This compact statement represents a virtual synopsis of the better-known poem about the role of "Woman Wisdom" in creation in Prov 8:22–31. Meanwhile, the first challenge to Job's effrontery in the theophanic speeches in Job 38–41 concerns creation (38:4–11):

> Where were you when I laid the earth's foundation? Tell me, if you understand.
> Who marked off its dimensions? Surely you know! Who stretched a measuring line across it?
> On what were its footings set, or who laid its cornerstone—
> while the morning stars sang together and all the angels shouted for joy?
> Who shut up the sea behind doors when it burst forth from the womb,
> when I made the clouds its garment and wrapped it in thick darkness,
> when I fixed limits for it and set its doors and bars in place,
> when I said, "This far you may come and no farther; here is where your proud waves halt"?

The idea of physical creation is clear enough, and many writers on the biblical wisdom literature emphasize, with good cause, that creation occupies the place of theological importance in the wisdom literature that redemption does in most of the rest of the OT, and furthermore, that it forms the basis for wisdom ethics.[11] What about the other "orders"?

The Sacral Order

This is a more original contribution to talk about natural orders. We could alternatively label it a spiritual order or a ceremonial order, yet the adjective sacral best captures the implication that spheres of life that we might today

---

11. Brown, *Wisdom's Wonder*, 16–17, is just one example.

see as utterly spiritually neutral bear directly on the worshipper's ceremonial standing before God, or upon the holiness of God itself. It offers a rubric for explaining how not just ethical and moral wrongs, but ceremonial infractions also, could "defile" the land of Israel and render it unsuitable for the nation's occupation. That is, it covers the whole system of purity, defilement, ceremonial ostracism, ceremonial purging, sacrificial atonement, restoration, and so forth.

Following long lists of sexual taboos in both Lev 18 and 20, we read warnings such as this from 20:22–23:

> Keep all my decrees and laws and follow them, so that the land where I am bringing you to live may not vomit you out. You must not live according to the customs of the nations I am going to drive out before you. Because they did all these things, I abhorred them. But I said to you, "You will possess their land; I will give it to you as an inheritance, a land flowing with milk and honey." I am the LORD your God, who has set you apart from the nations. You must therefore make a distinction between clean and unclean animals and between unclean and clean birds. Do not defile yourselves by any animal or bird or anything that moves along the ground—those that I have set apart as unclean for you. You are to be holy to me because I, the LORD, am holy, and I have set you apart from the nations to be my own.

The vital importance of this sacral holiness demands not just sexual restraint but restraint in contact with unclean bird species! This "spiritual order" may be foreign to many modern readers but would be more familiar to non-Western cultures (indigenous Australian culture comes to mind here) and is essential for grasping an Israelite, especially priestly, understanding of how access to and involvement with God must work. It explains a prophetic statement such as Jeremiah's: "'If a man divorces his wife and she leaves him and marries another man, should he return to her again? Would not the land be completely defiled? But you have lived as a prostitute with many lovers—would you now return to me?' declares the LORD" (Jer 3:1). Some present-day Christians might still question the ethics of frivolous divorce and remarriage, but in Jeremiah's oracle it is not just a moral or legal infraction but also a sacral issue, one of ceremonial or sacral defilement. Some writers would doubtless include this sacral concept under the heading of "moral order," but I make the distinction to help explain why it extends well beyond our common notion of morality.

PART I: ENGAGING ETHICALLY WITHIN CHRISTIAN COMMUNITY

Does this "sacral order" mind-set, however, extend into our biblical wisdom books? In OT scholarship about a generation ago there existed the widespread perception that biblical wisdom was inherently secular, a tradition adopted from Israel's wider ancient Near Eastern cultural context, and was only belatedly subject to a kind of theological editorial overlay in our biblical wisdom books.[12] Gerhard von Rad perceived this secularization in the narratives about David's reign in 2 Sam 6–20 and their corresponding (Solomonic) phase in Israelite society, an idea rejected by James Crenshaw and others.[13] Von Rad himself denies that he envisages any loss of "faith in Yahweh's power" on the part of wisdom teachers; the issue is rather one of desacralization, or the loss of the sacral perception of the world.[14] It might be helpful to clarify terms: my interest here is not to ask whether the wisdom literature is theological as opposed to secular; there is no question in my mind that it is theological through and through. The question is whether it is, we might say, mundane as opposed to sacral.[15]

I would concede that the sacral mind-set lies quite low in our wisdom literature, especially when compared with the priestly/sacrificial regime of Leviticus or the threat of defilement of the land in Deuteronomy.[16] However, it might be of value to point out a few places where this view of the world might show through. The understanding that dreams or night visions are capable of being revelatory or significant (in the sense of "signing" something), seen in Job 4:12–21 and 33:13–18, might be a sacral idea. Psalm 37, commonly recognized as a wisdom psalm or as having wisdom features, closely associates covenant fidelity and trust in the LORD with the privilege of land inheritance (vv. 3, 9, 11, 22, 27, 29, 34, and compare Matt 5:5).[17] The one obviously cultic passage in Ecclesiastes manifests a palpable

---

12. Crenshaw, *Old Testament Wisdom*, 92–93; Wilson, "Sacred and Profane," 318–22.

13. Rad, *Old Testament Theology*, 1:52–54; Rad, *Wisdom in Israel*, 58–60; Crenshaw, *Old Testament Wisdom*, 194, 260n.; Wilson, "Sacred and Profane," 315–18.

14. Rad, *Wisdom in Israel*, 60; Rad, *Old Testament Theology*, 1:53.

15. "Secular" originally meant "mundane" but has acquired a stronger sense as a kind of antonym to "religious," and this popular sense risks distorting the discussion about biblical wisdom literature.

16. See Deut 7:5, 25–26; 18:9–13. Note that the latter passage ends with the call to Israel to be blameless, the text that is the most likely OT referent if Jesus intends a scriptural allusion in Matt 5:48.

17. Crenshaw, *Old Testament Wisdom*, 181. Crenshaw here perceives a blending of wisdom and "ancient sacral traditions," attributing the land possession theme to the latter. This polarization seems a little inconsistent on Crenshaw's part, given that he generally de-emphasizes the sacred–secular divide in regards to wisdom.

sense of how dangerous it is to make frivolous vows to God and then negligently fail to fulfill them (Eccl 5:1–7). Finally, the element within Proverbs that directly attributes reward or punishment of human behavior to the conscious will of God (e.g., 16:4, 7, 9, 11) tends to align with a surviving sense of the sacral order, though it bears more directly with the idea of the moral order (see below). That is, the sacral mind-set probably forms a natural partner with a theistic retributive theology. Therefore I believe it is possible to say that the wisdom literature does not manifest a completely desacralized worldview.

The Social Order

This is another aspect of a "wisdom" view of the world that might sit uneasily with a modern audience steeped in democratic values, and it is the idea that the social order, with its family structures, social roles, leaders leading and servants serving, reflects God's creative handiwork also. Ancient Near Eastern creation myths such as Enuma Elish are only complete when the society concerned is operational, including with firmly established kingly rule and full service of the god/s established in the temple. Creation does not concern the physical order only, but also the social and spiritual. Ancient creation stories did not intend to explain just why there is a physical *earth*, but why there is a human *world*.

Any upsetting of the social order, then, was deeply unsettling to the ancient mind. To sample the thought of one who may be a non-Israelite speaker, we read in Prov 30:21–23: "Under three things the earth trembles, under four it cannot bear up: a servant who becomes king, a godless fool who gets plenty to eat, a contemptible woman who gets married, and a servant who displaces her mistress." We might wonder what is wrong with a little reversal of social status. European societies have a political history characterized by major revolutions that are often still viewed with much sympathy in the present day. How, in any case, could such social reversal affect the earth? Notice once again the implicit horror at this upheaval of social status:

> There is an evil I have seen under the sun,
> the sort of error that arises from a ruler:
> Fools are put in many high positions,
> while the rich occupy the low ones.

> I have seen slaves on horseback,
> while princes go on foot like slaves. (Eccl 10:5–7)

Perhaps we need to belong to a more traditional, even tribal society to instinctively resonate with this sort of moral outrage. Our instinctive desire might be for exactly such a reversal, unless it means the loss of our own personal privileges! Despite sentiments such as found in these wisdom texts, the OT also carries a countercultural theme of God's reversal of human social expectations, humbling the proud and esteeming the lowly.[18] We might revolt against understanding social status as God-given too, aware of the absolute monarchies sustained in early modern Europe by a doctrine of the divine right of kings, along with selfserving philosophies of social stratification maintained in more modern societies! The wisdom writers themselves emphasize that, if it comes to competing values, we should choose social humiliation rather than abandoning our personal integrity (Prov 16:19; 19:1, 22). Yet it remains important that we grasp the idea that human social structures fall within the parameters of creation from an OT and especially a wisdom standpoint, or else some of the statements we find in OT wisdom texts will make no sense to us. Note, for example, that Job's social humiliation represented for him the keenest of all his personal losses (Job 29:7—30:15).

The Moral Order

The busy discussion over the topic of a moral order in wisdom literature reveals a spectrum of views that corresponds to the spectrum in views over divine action in the natural world. In the latter case, it is possible, at one end, to think of God directly performing each natural event that occurs (a kind of occasionalism, to use a philosophical term), so that the term "natural law" has the minimal sense of "God's normal way of operating." The causative link between events on this account is more apparent than real, and we approach something like a *creatio continua*, a world remade at each moment according to the will of God. At the other extreme would be a world created with such a robust, independent existence that it can continue to function along natural, cause-and-effect lines without any intervention by God. In fact, a strong version of this end of the spectrum

---

18. Classically, in Hannah's Song in 1 Sam 2:1–10.

would essentially rule any intrusion by God into the causal network out-of-bounds. God can watch but cannot play.[19]

There are theological virtues and risks at each end of this "God and nature" discussion, but I mention this as an example to illustrate the spectrum that relates to moral order. Denial of a moral order would entail attributing any reward for right conduct or punishment for evil suggested in the Bible to the direct action of God. At the other end, a strong brand of moral order would regard the appropriate consequences for right and wrong conduct to be "built-in" to the moral fabric of the world, not requiring God's direct administration, but rather functioning automatically or semiautomatically. Klaus Koch's famous essay, "Is There a Doctrine of Retribution in the Old Testament?" advocated a rather strong version of this system of built-in consequences.[20]

Reading the wisdom books does at times give the impression that certain appropriate consequences *tend* to follow human behavior, whether virtuous or vicious. In some cases, these consequences sound quite natural, as if following the rules of general cause-and-effect: "Those who work their land will have abundant food, but those who chase fantasies have no sense" (Prov 12:11).[21] "Those who guard their lips preserve their lives, but those who speak rashly will come to ruin" (13:3). The first is a general rule of natural cause-and-effect tied to human behavior, while the second we might attribute to social cause-and-effect. Both would seem to operate without God's direct involvement.

Then there are statements of God's *direct* observation and repaying of conduct: "The eyes of the Lord are everywhere, keeping watch on the wicked and the good" (15:3). Or more basically, "The Lord works out everything to its proper end—even the wicked for a day of disaster" (16:4). More concretely, "The Lord tears down the house of the proud, but he sets the widow's boundary stone in place" (15:25). These verses suggest God's direct action to repay conduct according to its moral value.[22] Yet the last example shows

---

19. Van Till, "Basil, Augustine," 21–38, goes rather close to this position, in my opinion.

20. This leads him to answer his own question "no," based on his presumption that the term "retribution" implied God's direct dealing of judgment. However, the meaning of the term "retribution" need not be limited to the interventionist end of the spectrum. Koch, "Doctrine of Retribution," 57–87; Klaus Koch, "Gibt es ein Vergeltungsdogma?," 1–42.

21. The following quotations are all from Proverbs.

22. Koch seems to underplay such references in his interest to show the automatic

that such direct action cannot be *unmediated* action, unless we can imagine the proud person's house collapsing spontaneously (this being a regular phenomenon), or a widow's boundary stone, unjustly shifted, migrating back into place before our eyes like a Death Valley boulder.

We are led, therefore, to a third class of statements that might imply a kind of fundamental moral fabric or order to the world that inherently tends to resist evil and expedite righteousness. "The path of the righteous is like the morning sun, shining ever brighter till the full light of day. But the way of the wicked is like deep darkness; they do not know what makes them stumble" (4:18–19). Such references could be multiplied from the wisdom books. Proverbs, in particular, embodies this paradigm of a *moral law* of cause-and-effect that operates in the world. Individuals may work "with the system" by living righteously, and *generally* prosper as a result, or fight the system by living foolishly and/or maliciously and find themselves resisted at every turn. It is those who go against the grain who get splinters: "The righteousness of the blameless makes their paths straight, but the wicked are brought down by their own wickedness" (11:5). Thus, Timothy Sandoval concludes, "Hence, those who attain wisdom's virtues and thus align themselves with the genuine nature of the wisdom-infused cosmos ought not be surprised if they reap real-life well-being."[23]

What might be the risks of embracing a strong "moral order" perspective for ourselves? It could easily become a belief in karma, which is essentially a rigid, automatic, and impersonal system of retribution. It might render our image of God remote and uninvolved, unable to tinker with the machine. It might prove so untrue to lived experience as to be unworkable. The difficult life of a *dalit* or "untouchable" person in Indian society is a warning of the social consequences of such a view. Karma is very reassuring for the powerful and prosperous, but disempowering if it is not. Christians have become grateful acquaintances of grace. We do not lightly forget what it is to receive more than we deserve.

God has granted us in Scripture a kind of "trialogue" between Proverbs, Job, and Ecclesiastes over retribution. Whereas Proverbs says that honesty (diligence, godliness, prudence, kindness, justice, etc.) is the best policy, Ecclesiastes counters, "During the days of my fleeting life I have seen both of these things: Sometimes a righteous person dies prematurely in spite of his righteousness, and sometimes a wicked person lives long in spite

---

nature of the system according to the wisdom writings.

23. Sandoval, "Proverbs," 103.

of his evil deeds" (Eccl 7:15, NET). And the lamenting Job adds, "True, just look at me!" Yet while Leo Perdue and others would present this as a fundamental clash of worldviews between "traditional" and "critical" sages,[24] I feel that there is a creative tension here that provides the reader of the Bible with a multifaceted glimpse of the truth about acts and consequences. Truth is three-dimensional, and just as the facets of a diamond might stand opposite one another, such creative tension is often necessary if we are to grasp the truths of a complex life in God's world.

Thus, with suitable caution, and for the sake of biblical understanding, we take on board for consideration the suggestion that the biblical wisdom writers are sometimes assuming, sometimes questioning, but nevertheless frequently engaging the idea that there is a moral fabric to the world that might help to explain why there is any pattern of moral consequences at all. A vital last point is to remember that these orders are presented as deeply interconnected, not compartmentalized, which is why the natural order might suffer when the moral order is transgressed, or the social order disrupted, as seen in the examples already offered.

The Creation Path to Ethics in the Wisdom Literature

To return to Timothy Sandoval's summary of the ethical stance of Proverbs, the moral order of the world is part of its created status. "According to Prov. 8:22–31, wisdom is intimately related to Yahweh's act of creation and might be said to infuse creation itself."[25] Job 28 describes wisdom via the metaphor of a precious resource for which one might mine, and concludes that wisdom is not so much *under* every created thing as *in* it:

> God understands the way to it and he alone knows where it dwells, for he views the ends of the earth and sees everything under the heavens. When he established the force of the wind and measured out the waters, when he made a decree for the rain and a path for the thunderstorm, then he looked at wisdom and appraised it; he confirmed it and tested it. And he said to the human race, "The fear of the Lord—that is wisdom, and to shun evil is understanding." (Job 28:23–28)

---

24. Perdue, "Ethics of Wisdom Literature," 87–94.
25. Sandoval, "Proverbs," 103. Cf. Prov 3:19–20 once again.

PART I: ENGAGING ETHICALLY WITHIN CHRISTIAN COMMUNITY

An effectively created world will be inherently orderly, like a well-ruled kingdom. Therefore, it makes sense to read, just a few verses prior to Woman Wisdom's song of creation in Prov 8:22–31, "By me kings reign and rulers issue decrees that are just; by me princes govern, and nobles—all who rule on earth." Social order, moral order, natural order—all grounded in the creative initiative of God.

Human ethical responsibility, therefore, is the responsibility of a creature toward its creator. Such a basis for ethics is inherently broader than, though complementary to, a covenantal basis for ethics that operates out of God's election and saving work. It matches the universal feel of the wisdom writings, which are as international as the over-the-border setting of the dialogues in Job[26] or the meditations of the non-Israelite King Lemuel (Prov 31). The qualifier here is that biblical wisdom is never international to the point of polytheism! The dialogues of Job might carefully avoid Israel's covenant name for God, Yahweh,[27] but none of the friends consider the competing programs of rival deities as a possible explanation for Job's perplexing situation. It can only be interpreted with reference to this sole God. So wisdom ethics, like covenant ethics, finds its basis in the person of God, but is differently derived, via creation rather than covenant.

In the vertical dimension, then, to be created obliges the creature to revere God and to recognize God's fundamental ownership of and authority over him/herself. The wisdom books establish no separation between godly conduct and ethical conduct. They instead present worship and reverence as the righteous ethic relevant to the vertical dimension of life. This is the "fear of God" urged in Job 28:28, Prov 1:7 and 9:10, Eccl 12:1, 13, and Ps 111:10. It is not what you know, but who you know; it is not possible to fathom wisdom by mining for it, but it is possible to discover relationship with the Ultimately Wise, the author of all order. The call to "fear God and keep His commands"[28] has been deemed by some an artificial final gesture appended to a skeptical book; appended it might be, but the book's "live for the moment" philosophy still incorporates the fear of God as a fundamental value (11:7–10). Meanwhile, Proverbs has been suspected not of skepticism so much as secularity, a system of profitable living rather independent from

---

26. Biblical associations of "Uz" (Job 1:1) are Edomite and/or Aramean or possibly Arabian (Gen 10:23 // 1 Chr 1:17; Gen 22:21; Gen 36:28 // 1 Chr 1:42; Jer 25:23), while Teman, the home town of Eliphaz, is in Edom.

27. Job 12:9 is the lonely exception that proves the rule in Job 3–37.

28. Eccl 12:13, HCSB.

spiritual considerations. Yet the context preceding the creation and wisdom statement in 3:19–20 is full of connections between fear of the LORD and the righteous life, and the theistic undertone of even the practical proverb collection in chapters 10–31 is unmistakable. Prior to any choosing or calling, the very gift of the chance of life through creation is more than enough warrant for worship of the Creator.

A creation-based ethics then recognizes its obligations in the horizontal, interpersonal dimension. If covenantal ethics recognizes one's obligation to support God's gift of the privileges of covenant membership to one's neighbor, such as land rights and legal protection in the case of Israel, then a creation-based ethics recognizes the high privilege that it is for each fellow human, each living creature, even inanimate parts of creation, to be created by God. In the case of humanity, this hinges on the recognition that not just "humanity" as a generic category, and not just the original humans, but *each individual human* is created by God. It is surprising how low-profile this idea is in systematic theology. Whole volumes of systematic theology sometimes lack any reference to it.[29] Can we be confident that this is a biblical tenet of belief? Psalm 139 leaps to mind with its "fearfully and wonderfully made," whose seventeenth-century phrasing has become embedded in our theological vocabulary. Well and good, but the wisdom literature amplifies this theme along with its ethical consequences. Job 10:8–12, 18 lament the incongruity of having been personally shaped and lovingly "curdled" like a quality French cheese only to be gratuitously destroyed. Now not every opinion uttered in these angsty dialogues receives implicit canonical endorsement as a received doctrine. Yet the reader of Job 10 senses that this view of the individual human deserves that kind of credit. This is how Job draws out the implications of individual creation for ethical relationships in his final testament of righteousness in chapters 29–31:

> If I have denied justice to any of my servants, whether male or female, when they had a grievance against me, what will I do when God confronts me? What will I answer when called to account? Did not he who made me in the womb make them? Did not the same one form us both within our mothers? (Job 31:13–15)

In an ancient world where slaves were typically viewed as property and protected only as a material asset, this creation ethic intrudes to defend

---

29. I speak from experience of searching for it. Some welcome exceptions are: Wolff, *Anthropology*, 93–98; Brown, "*Creatio Corporis*," 107–9; Soskice, "Creation and Relation," 31–39.

the human rights of fellow creatures. Given that "rich and poor have this in common: the LORD is the Maker of them all" (Prov 22:2) and that "the poor and the oppressor have this in common: the LORD gives sight to the eyes of both" (Prov 29:13) then it follows that "whoever oppresses the poor shows contempt for their Maker, but whoever is kind to the needy honors God" (Prov 14:31; cf. 17:5). It is this creation-based ethical mandate that underlies the specific ethical behaviors advocated in the wisdom literature, as illustrated in Table 1:[30]

Table 1

Principle	Job Text	Proverbs Text	Ecclesiastes Text
Piety towards God	28:28; 31:26–28	3:1–12; 15:33—16:5	12:1, 6, 12–14
Prizing of wisdom	28:20–27	Chs. 1–9	8:1; 9:17–18
Just use of authority	31:38–40	8:12–16; 31:1–9	10:16–17
Generous use of wealth	29:12–17; 31:16–20	17:5; 19:17; 22:9	11:1–2
Just conduct in court	31:13–15, 21–22	17:15, 23, 26; 31:8–9	3:16; 5:8–9; 8:11, 14
Fidelity in marriage	31:1–4, 9–12	5:1–23; 7:1–27	9:9
Integrity in speech	31:29–30	17:20, 27–28; 18:4–8	5:2–7; 10:12–13
Diligence in work	29:7?	6:6–11; 18:9	9:10; 10:18; 11:1–6
Humility instead of pride	40:11–12	16:5, 18–19; 18:12	7:1–8
Sincerity instead of hypocrisy	31:33–34	4:24–27; 12:17–22	7:16–18?
Contentment instead of coveting	22:23–26	15:16–17; 17:1; 23:4–5	5:10–12

30. Ecclesiastes maintains the habit of qualifying the value of the virtues it describes insofar as they do not guarantee good life outcomes for their possessors nor provide a way to avoid death. This kind of qualification does not equate to complete nullification of all value.

Nothing in this table is inconsistent with the conduct towards others demanded by one's covenant obligations to God, but the theological basis in creation represents a different rationale for such conduct.

The Distinctive Contributions of the Old Testament Wisdom Books

Each of our canonical wisdom books is quite distinct from the others, so we cannot claim to have surveyed their contribution to our biblical understanding of ethics until we consider each one in itself.

Proverbs: Ethical Practicality

The ethical paradigm presented in Proverbs is the most systematic in the wisdom literature, with a programmatic prologue (chs. 1–9) and a large collection of proverbial "raw material" in chapters 10–31. Sandoval reports the objection of Wolfgang Mieder that a presumed original oral context is vital to a proverb's viability, so that "a proverb in a collection is dead."[31] This is too negative. True, reading the proverbs en masse is a difficult task, because a written collection is not their natural environment. Yet I suspect that the budding sage had the task of studying and memorizing them en masse and by rote in order to have them available for application later as a labor of sapiential investment.[32] A proverb in a collection is not dead; it is a seed awaiting planting in new soil, the soil of a new situation and a new audience.

We value the practicality of Proverbs—practicality, rather than simply pragmatism. Its truths are not pertinent to every reader at every moment, but to some reader at every moment, and every reader at some moment. We read observations such as "Like cold water to a weary soul is good news from a distant land" (Prov 25:25) and know that they reflect real experiences such as we have known. We read, "A man who does not control his temper is like a city whose wall is broken down" (25:28, HCSB) and, with a little unpacking of the metaphor, might think of somebody we have met in the past. Proverbs invites right living toward God arising from an attitude of faithfulness, right living toward others that manifests a spirit of fairness, and in fact right living towards oneself, advising that wise and righteous

---

31. Sandoval, "Proverbs," 101.
32. Toorn, *Scribal Culture*, 80–84; Carr, *Formation*, 408–10.

conduct really is good for you. Is it naively optimistic? No. The numerous protests against ethical evil and assurances that the perpetrators' day is coming, for example, "When the wicked thrive, so does sin, but the righteous will see their downfall" (29:16), necessarily imply that good people may expect to suffer for a season. There is a genuine realism in Proverbs for those with eyes to see it.

Job: Ethical Integrity

> If I have put my trust in gold
> or said to pure gold, "You are my security,"
> if I have rejoiced over my great wealth,
> the fortune my hands had gained,
> if I have regarded the sun in its radiance
> or the moon moving in splendor,
> so that my heart was secretly enticed
> and my hand offered them a kiss of homage,
> then these also would be sins to be judged,
> for I would have been unfaithful to God on high. (Job 31:24–28)

If we conceive the story of Job as an unwitting trial, chapter 31 constitutes his final oath of innocence, a kind of self-righteous statutory declaration. With that his testimony is complete and the trial moves toward its conclusion. The chapter consists of a series of self-imprecatory oaths, should Job be guilty of any of a series of ethical crimes. These include the critically important, yet, in terms of OT ethics, expected concern for the poor and vulnerable, and that not just as an ideal in theory, but implemented in active help and just legal process (31:16–23). Yet the ethical scope of this chapter ranges far beyond such observable and measurable external behaviors to matters of personal integrity subject only to the scrutiny of God: avoidance of lust (vv. 1, 9), dishonest motives (v. 5), materialism (vv. 24–25), secret worship of sun or moon (vv. 26–27), or quietly celebrating the downfall of a personal enemy (vv. 29–30)! Such a standard of personal integrity, extending well beyond the reach of public examination, is perhaps unrivalled in the OT, reminding us of the impossible-sounding ideal of the Sermon on the Mount, "Be perfect, therefore, as your heavenly Father is perfect" (Matt 5:48).[33] Job 31:33 highlights the issue of concealed

---

33. As touched upon earlier, my own feeling is that other English lemmas beside the popular (i.e., entrenched) choice "perfect" could be considered in order to best convey the nuances of the Greek τέλειος into English here. "Pure in heart" from earlier in the

sin as a core concern. This is an apt reminder in an age whose mood is to limit moral critique only to those external actions that directly affect other people. Job is not content to assert consistency in his ethical actions; he declares the clarity of his moral motivations.

Using the term "self-righteous" of Job raises the question of pride or conceit here. We can hardly imagine any living person having such spotless integrity, making Job's avowals of innocence here and throughout the dialogues (chs. 3–27) look dishonest or self-deceiving. This conundrum forces us to clarify our understanding of the genre of the book of Job. Are we dealing with historical narrative here? Did one of the three friends prove particularly diligent as a stenographer and record this extended conversation? Was Job the one completely honest citizen of the ancient Near East? It is certainly possible, even likely, that the experiences of a prominent citizen of the ancient world provided the inspiration for the book. It is also clear on a careful reading, and with awareness of the literary use of the dialogue form from Plato down through to Galileo and Hume, that dialogues are a long-recognized way of putting rival understandings of reality onto the playing field and letting them compete. Thus, John Walton uses an apt label when he calls Job a "thought experiment," that is, a theological test case.[34] What if there was a person of spotless integrity, yet who suffered greatly? Where would be the justice of God in that? Would that person keep worshipping God if there was no expectation of personal benefit? Does "disinterested" worship in this sense exist anywhere, or is every manifestation of religion some version of a cargo cult? These are the kinds of questions being addressed in this book.

Walton insightfully explains Job's dogged defense of his own innocence in another writing, helping us to understand why this defense does not constitute "self-righteousness" in the pejorative sense. What we might take as Job's stubborn resistance to self-examination is actually the crucial mark of his integrity throughout the dialogues. If he has done nothing to deserve his suffering, and that is exactly what chapter 1 tells us, then it would be a failure of integrity to enter into confession before God. It would be to fall into the

---

chapter (Matt 5:8) corresponds well to the sense of the term, yet we are reluctant to translate a single word with a three word phrase or to obscure the distinction that exists between the terms used in these two places. Considering the entire chapter-length discussion in Pennington's book on the Sermon on the Mount, my suggestion would be, "Therefore be *true*, as your Father in Heaven is *true*." See Pennington, *Sermon on the Mount*, 69–85.

34. Walton, *Job*, 26.

temptation to engage in appeasement of the deity for the sake of material restoration. This would only prove the Accuser's jibe in the prologue, that no such thing as disinterested,[35] sincere worship of God exists, only worship performed for material reward (1:9–11; 2:4–5). Job thus concludes his part in the dialogues with determination: "I will maintain my innocence and never let go of it; my conscience will not reproach me as long as I live" (Job 27:6). Should he flinch here by confessing sins he does not truly believe he has committed, the Accuser wins the wager. "[H]e will not simply offer a blanket, blind confession with the hopes that he will appease God's inexplicable wrath and be restored to prosperity."[36] What, then, is Job confessing when he finally admits error and "repents" (42:6)?[37] He is not admitting moral or ethical failures in his life *prior to* his crisis that warranted the suffering he experienced. He is admitting that in his extremity he overstepped the mark in his speech *within* the dialogues and, forced by his own retribution theology to find fault in someone for his suffering, condemns God in order to justify himself (40:8).[38] This accounts for the plainly reproving tone of the Yahweh speeches in chapters 38–41, while allowing for God's verdict in the final frame that in some sense Job has responded rightly to God in contrast to his friends (42:8).

What then is the unique contribution of the book of Job to the ethics of OT wisdom? The book reminds us that the kind of reward and retribution pattern that might either be observed at work in daily life, inferred from the perception of a moral order in God's created world, or indeed read out of Proverbs or Deuteronomy or the histories of Israel, has many, mysterious exceptions. Neither suffering nor prosperity have prior merit as their sole possible cause. There are many other reasons why we might experience fortune or misfortune, for example, in this case a heavenly wager, making it impossible to read back from a person's current situation to their ethical standing. Because the moral order does not produce reward and retribution like a cosmic vending machine, and a person might experience

---

35. Again, I use the term "disinterested" in its more technical usage of an action not motivated by the prospect of personal gain.

36. Walton, "Job 1: Book of," 338.

37. There is significant scholarly debate over the meaning of Job 42:6; the best explanation of the available alternatives in my view is that of Clines, *Job 38–42*, 1208–11, 1218–23.

38. Walton, "Job 1: Book of," 339. I consider this article a very effective treatment of the meaning of the book of Job and would highly recommend it. It is a deeply understood and profound handling of a profound biblical book.

in the present the exact opposite of what he or she apparently deserves, ethical conduct cannot hinge on any certainty of lifestyle benefits and must extend to situations no one but God can see. The surest basis of ethical conduct is not the hope of future reward, but authentic devotion to God such as modeled by Job. What is the anchor for such devotion? It is that God is worth it. That is the key to the wager in Job, and that is the true warrant for worship. Does Job fall away from his devotion in the severity of his struggle? No. While Job puzzles and grieves over the workings of the moral order, he does not merely wonder to himself, nor complain to his friends. His complaints in most of his speeches soon turn Godward. He puzzles in prayer, and that is the mark of a living devotion.

Ecclesiastes: Ethical Durability

Compared to the prayerfulness of the book of Job, we might feel that Ecclesiastes breathes a more secular air. The thinker on center stage here, who goes by the name Qoheleth on the basis of the Hebrew text ("Teacher," 1:12), talks about God rather than to him. Yet this is partly a function of a genre difference. Ecclesiastes is neither a dialogue nor a prayer, but a reflection on the meaning of life in God's world and indeed a meta-reflection, turning at times to consider the value of the wisdom process of doing such reflection. At first reading, the Teacher presents us with a perspective that is both refreshing in its realism and dispiriting in its sense of futility. Work is toil (8:15–16). Joy is passing, and so is youth (11:9–10). Wealth is easily lost, grand achievements will pass, and heroic deeds will soon be forgotten (9:16). We cannot count on getting what we deserve, or even what our gifts and talents might predict; "The race is not to the swift, or the battle to the strong . . . but time and chance happen to them all" (9:11).

Some have concluded therefore that Ecclesiastes is deeply pessimistic. Yet it is pessimistic only about certain values, such as the habit of turning the present into toil and sorrow in the hope of cashing in at a future time (4:4, 8).[39] Qoheleth would query the "frenetic tourist" approach to life that travels the globe and visits lookouts over spectacular views, only to spend ten minutes frantically taking photographs for posterity before reboarding the tourist bus. Qoheleth does not say that life is worthless, but, given our fundamental restrictions as humans having no insight into the future, no

---

39. For this optimistic reading of Ecclesiastes, see especially Brown, *Wisdom's Wonder*, 159–83.

certainty of prosperity or recognition, no access to the plans of God (3:11), we must not continually plug our present earnings back into the slot machine in the hope of a brighter future. It is the gift of God to "eat and drink and find satisfaction in [one's] toil" in the present moment (3:13). How do we know that this is not a call to self-indulgence and a "devil-may-care" attitude, even to ethical living? Ecclesiastes never ceases to remind us: "God will call the past to account."[40] That God cares to judge each deed gives the momentary and transient everlasting significance. It is only in the eternity of God that any slice of mortal life can gain transcendent significance. Much that we might normally rely on will prove ephemeral. Yet ethical righteousness, though it cannot prevent us from dying (9:1–6), makes an eternal impression on the mind of God.

Conclusion

The OT wisdom books make a vital and unique contribution to a biblically generated ethical model. That they do not operate out of a primarily covenantal framework allows them to contribute ethical concepts that do not presuppose delivery of a divine law or a long, corporate experience of national deliverance at the hand of God. Yet they remain theistic, and do not describe a universe that generates reward or retribution of human conduct independent of the will of a supreme God. Their anchorage is in the creative rather than the redemptive work of God. Presuming orders that structure the world on not only physical but also sacral, moral, and social levels, they challenge the hearer to consider whether his or her own course of life benefits from working "with the grain" of those orders, or really, that single, multifaceted order. Lest this order be perceived too rigidly, guaranteeing reward or punishment in the present experience of life in perfect correspondence to one's behavior, both Job and Ecclesiastes in their unique ways remind us that a sovereign God retains the right to either dispense or withhold reward or punishment for his own reasons, reasons that may have nothing to do with individual merit. Our integrity must not survive simply in the hope of suitable reward; it must ultimately derive solely from an authentic reverence for God and God's inherent worth, in the hope that whether we suffer or prosper, "the works of God might be displayed in [us]" (John 9:3).

---

40. Eccl 3:15a; see also 3:17; 9:1; 11:7–10; 12:1, 8, 14.

Bibliography

Birch, Bruce C. "Ethics in the Old Testament." In *The New Interpreter's Dictionary of the Bible*, edited by Katherine Doob Sakenfeld, 2:338–48. Nashville: Abingdon, 2007.

Brown, William P. "*Creatio Corporis* and the Rhetoric of Defense in Job 10 and Psalm 139." In *God Who Creates: Essays in Honor of W. Sibley Towner*, edited by William P. Brown and S. Dean McBride, 107–24. Grand Rapids: Eerdmans, 2000.

———. *Wisdom's Wonder: Character, Creation, and Crisis in the Bible's Wisdom Literature*. Grand Rapids: Eerdmans, 2014.

Carr, David M. *The Formation of the Hebrew Bible: A New Reconstruction*. New York: Oxford University Press, 2011.

Clines, David J. A. *Job 38–42*. New ed. WBC 18B. Grand Rapids: Zondervan, 2015.

Crenshaw, James L. *Old Testament Wisdom: An Introduction*. Atlanta: John Knox, 1981.

Green, Joel B., and Jacqueline E. Lapsley, eds. *The Old Testament and Ethics: A Book-By-Book Survey*. Grand Rapids: Baker Academic, 2013.

Koch, Klaus. "Gibt es ein Vergeltungsdogma im Alten Testament?" *ZTK* 52, no. 1 (1955) 1–42.

———. "Is There a Doctrine of Retribution in the Old Testament." In *Theodicy in the Old Testament*, edited by James Crenshaw, 57–87. Philadelphia: Fortress, 1983.

Pennington, Jonathan T. *The Sermon on the Mount and Human Flourishing: A Theological Commentary*. Grand Rapids: Baker Academic, 2017.

Perdue, Leo G. "Cosmology and the Social Order in the Wisdom Tradition." In *The Sage in Israel and the Ancient Near East*, edited by John G. Gammie and Leo G. Perdue, 457–78. Winona Lake: Eisenbrauns, 1990.

———. "Ethics of Wisdom Literature." In *The Old Testament and Ethics: A Book-By-Book Survey*, edited by Joel B. Green and Jacqueline E. Lapsley, 87–94. Grand Rapids: Baker Academic, 2013.

Sandoval, Timothy J. "Proverbs." In *The Old Testament and Ethics: A Book-By-Book Survey*, edited by Joel B. Green and Jacqueline E. Lapsley, 100–104. Grand Rapids: Baker Academic, 2013.

Seow, Choon-Leong. "Job." In *The Old Testament and Ethics: A Book-By-Book Survey*, edited by Joel B. Green and Jacqueline E. Lapsley, 94–97. Grand Rapids: Baker Academic, 2013.

Soskice, Janet. "Creation and Relation." *Theology* 94 (1991) 31–39.

Toorn, Karel van der. *Scribal Culture and the Making of the Hebrew Bible*. Cambridge: Harvard University Press, 2007.

Van Till, H. J. "Basil, Augustine and the Doctrine of Creation's Functional Integrity." *Science and Christian Belief* 8 (1996) 21–38.

VanDrunen, David. "Wisdom and the Natural Moral Order: The Contribution of Proverbs to a Christian Theology of Natural Law." *Journal of the Society of Christian Ethics* 33, no. 1 (2013) 153–68.

Rad, Gerhard von. *Old Testament Theology*. 2 vols. Edinburgh: Oliver & Boyd, 1965.

———. *Wisdom in Israel*. Nashville: Abingdon, 1972.

Walton, John H. "Job 1: Book of." In *Dictionary of the Old Testament: Wisdom, Poetry and Writings*, edited by Tremper Longman III and Peter Enns, 333–46. Downers Grove: InterVarsity, 2008.

———. *Job*. NIV Application Commentary. Grand Rapids: Zondervan, 2012.

Wilson, Frederick M. "Sacred and Profane: The Yahwistic Redaction of Proverbs Reconsidered." In *The Listening Heart: Essays in Wisdom and the Psalms in Honor of Roland E Murphy, O Carm*, 313–34. JSOTSup 58. Sheffield: Sheffield Academic, 1987.

Wolff, Hans Walter. *Anthropology of the Old Testament*. Philadelphia: Augsburg Fortress, 1974.

Wright, Christopher J. H. *God's People in God's Land*. Grand Rapids: Eerdmans, 1990.

———. *Old Testament Ethics for the People of God*. Nottingham: InterVarsity, 2004.

2

Deciding about Deciding

*Early Christian Communal
Decision-Making in Acts*

Steve Walton

RACHEL DOLEZAL IS A woman in the United States who caused—and causes—great controversy because of her self-identification as a black woman. She was elected president of the Spokane chapter of the National Association for the Advancement of Colored People in 2014, and this led in June 2015 to a major controversy after she was asked whether her parents were African American in a press interview, and walked out rather than answering. It turned out that her parents were both white, and her parents later said that she had "disguise[d] herself" as African American.[1] When photographed at age eighteen, her skin was pale and freckled, and she was unquestionably white; now her skin is significantly darker. When pressed on this, Dolezal said that she considered herself to be black. In a television interview in November 2015, she acknowledged that she was born white, but said, "I acknowledge that I was biologically born white to white parents, but I identify as black."[2] More recently, in a February 2017 interview with

---

1. Mosendz, "Family Accuses NAACP Leader."
2. Frizell, "Rachel Dolezal."

the UK newspaper *The Guardian*, she said that racial identity "wasn't even biological to begin with. *It was always a social construct.*"³

I am telling you Dolezal's story not to comment on the rights or wrongs of it, but to illustrate a key feature of the postmodern world in which we Westerners live. People wish to self-identify on the basis of how they see themselves, and identity is seen as an "inner" quality of a person, rather than something seen because of their external features, body characteristics, or family origins. This view locates identity in the private, individual sphere rather than the public sphere, and represents a historical shift from how people predominantly have been seen and understood. In some ways it could be liberating, for it gives people the opportunity not to be defined by their family or their family's past. The point to notice here is not whether it is particularly good or bad, but that it is a symptom of this wider movement concerning human identity.

Some years ago, I asked a Kenyan student whom I taught in Nottingham what major differences he noticed between British culture and his native culture in Kenya, and his response was fascinating. He said that Kenyans think of themselves as "we" first, whereas (white) British people think of themselves as "I" first. I think that's an accurate observation, at least about British people. This individualization affects many, many areas of modern Western culture, and it particularly affects our decision-making. We want the freedom to make decisions and to (as we say) "think for ourselves"—indeed, our education systems encourage such individual thinking and reflection. This has an impact on church culture, where the predominant way that Protestants, and increasingly Catholics too, make decisions about the church they will join—or leave—is about how "at home" they feel there.⁴ People have adopted a consumerist, "shopping mall" attitude, that of all the options around, at this period of their life they want to self-identify as Pentecostal or Anglican or Vineyard, etc.—or even, that they want to identify with a particular local church within a wider grouping because it has a particular theological and cultural flavor. The key thing to notice is that this is an *individual* choice or, at most, a nuclear family choice.

Such an approach to decision-making is historically unusual, and does not reflect the culture of the ancient texts found in the Bible. In particular, when we engage with the book of Acts, a book that perhaps more than any

---

3. Aitkenhead, "Rachel Dolezal," my italics.

4. For example, consider the phenomenon of the growth of the traditional Latin mass among young people in the West, e.g., Lyman, "Latin Mass."

other New Testament book shows us how the earliest believers went about their decision-making on major and minor topics, we encounter a different culture and a different approach to decision-making. That is the approach I shall explore in this chapter.

We shall look at this through first noticing the communal nature of the believing community in Acts, and then through studying some specific examples of decision-making. We shall notice some common features to these decision-making processes, and then look in more detail at the major decision about the terms on which non-Jewish people were to be allowed to participate as members of the believing community.

The Importance of the Communal in Acts

In line with their Jewish heritage, the earliest believers acted and lived communally. We can see this particularly in the early chapters of Acts, where Luke sketches key features of their shared life, notably in 2:42–47:

> They were devoting themselves to the apostles' teaching and the fellowship, the breaking of bread, and the prayers. Fear kept coming on everyone, and many wonders and signs were taking place through the apostles. All those who had come to believe were together and they used to hold everything as common; they used to sell their possessions and belongings and distribute the proceeds to all, as anyone had need. Day by day, spending much time together in the temple and breaking bread in homes, they shared food with joy and singleness of heart, praising God and having favour with the whole people. Every day the Lord was adding to their group those being saved.[5]

Throughout this section, the verbs are plural, denoting the shared life of the community. Indeed, the community are "the fellowship" (κοινωνία, *koinōnia*, v. 42), which involved daily meetings and a commitment to sharing material resources. This sharing is not unnatural within Middle Eastern culture, but Luke presents it in terms that echo the highest aspirations of both Jewish Scripture and Greco-Roman writings (vv. 44–45 with 4:32–35).[6] The believers included diaspora Jews who remained in Jerusalem after Pentecost (2:9–11), Galilean disciples and apostles, and urban Jerusalemites, both wealthy and poor. This diversity highlights a contrast with

---

5. My translation, as are other translations from the NT in this chapter.
6. See Walton, "Communism," 103–5.

Greco-Roman approaches to sharing possessions, for they were limited to those of equal (normally high) social status—here the needs of believers in poverty are met through their wealthier sisters and brothers.

Specifically, the shared meals happened in public and private (as we would say). Verse 46 portrays their shared meals as taking place both in homes and in the temple. Notice the way that two participial clauses "spending much time together" (προσκαρτεροῦντες ὁμοθυμαδὸν ἐν τῷ ἱερῷ, *proskarterountes homothymadon en tō hierō*) and "breaking bread in homes" (κλῶντές . . . κατ' οἶκον ἄρτον, *klōntes . . . kat' oikon arton*) are dependent on the same main verb "they shared food" (μετελάμβανον τροφῆς, *metelambanon trophēs*). Thus some of their meals took place in public space, probably in Solomon's Portico, a part of the temple complex that was covered and where they met (Acts 5:12)—perhaps in imitation of Jesus's own practice of teaching in the temple.

Two more passages in the early part of Acts underline this common life. Acts 4:32–35 reiterates and develops the earlier portrait, and in particular, verse 34 echoes Deut 15:4–5:

> There was no-one in need among them (Acts 4:34).

> There will, however, *be no one in need among you*, because the LORD is sure to bless you in the land that the LORD your God is giving you as a possession to occupy, if only you will obey the LORD your God by diligently observing this entire commandment that I command you today. (Deut 15:4–5, my italics)

Luke portrays the life of the early community as fulfilling hopes for the shared life of Israel. In this respect the believers resembled the Essene communities dotted around Palestine who met evening by evening and pooled the money they had gained from working that day in order to buy food, which they then ate together.[7] However, by contrast with the strictness of the residential Essene community at Qumran, the pooling of goods among the believers was not compulsory—people gave as they were able.[8] Note, however, that "community" was not a vague thing, but highly practical. Acts 4:32–35 prepares for the following two passages, where Barnabas is pictured as a positive example of sharing (4:36–37), and Ananias and Sapphira, who lie about what they are giving to the community, are a negative example (5:1–11). A further summary follows (5:12–16) that repeats

---

7. Philo, *Hypoth.* 1.10–11.
8. See my discussion in "Communism," 106–8.

the message of shared meetings in the temple area (v. 12b), and focuses on the "signs and wonders" happening through the apostles.

Not only this, but even when a dispute happens, it is as *a result of their shared community life*. The argument about the care for widows in 6:1–6 could not have happened had the Hebrew and Hellenistic believers never met together, for they would not have known of the practices of each other's groups. Their disagreement suggests that the two language groups met as one, at least some of the time (most likely in the larger meetings in the temple courts), and that when teaching was given, interpretation was provided for those who could not understand the language used.

To read these passages is naturally to be provoked to ask what happened later in the life of the believing community, since such immediate economic sharing did not continue. Luke himself goes on, however, to describe other forms of economic sharing among believers, including between communities of believers.[9] The Antiochene believers sent to the Jerusalem believers at a time of famine (11:27–30). Dorcas is commended as one who contributed by making clothes for widows (9:36, 39). Paul provides for himself and his companions through his physical work (18:3; 20:34). Paul asserts that he does not desire others' goods (20:33), but rather seeks to support the weak (20:35), a practice that he presents to the Ephesian elders for their imitation. As an example, Paul pays the hairdressing expenses of a group of Jewish believers who take a vow (21:23–24, 26). This variety of forms of economic sharing as expressions of response to the gospel is in tune with Paul's own teaching in 2 Cor 8–9, where his call for generous giving is rooted in God's generous giving in Christ (8:9), and his invitation to the Corinthians is that their surplus should provide for others in need (8:13–14). In sum, it seems that the principle that believers should be ready to share economically with their sisters and brothers in need underlay a "mixed economy" of expressions of that principle.

So what about Paul? We tend to think of him as the great individualist, the great "lone ranger" among the apostles. But is that an accurate portrait? Notice two features that suggest otherwise.

First, Paul regularly has coworkers traveling with him who provide a "support group," and are part of his mission team.[10] For example, when he leaves Antioch for the first time, Barnabas goes with him—indeed at this point, Barnabas seems to take the lead, for he is named first (13:2). We also

---

9. More fully, see my student Fiona Gregson's work: Gregson, *Everything*, ch. 3.
10. See the helpful brief article, Ellis, "Coworkers."

learn that John Mark also goes with them and acts as their assistant (13:5), although at some point he abandons them and returns home (15:38). When Paul wants to set out to visit the churches he has planted on that first trip, his first instinct is to take a companion, Barnabas, but when they cannot agree over taking John Mark, Paul takes Silas (15:36–40). Paul later adds Timothy to the team in Lystra (16:1–4), and he is part of the group that plants the church in Thessalonica (1 Thess 1:1).[11] Throughout Paul's travels from here the group is plural, either described as "they" (e.g., 16:6–8) or "we" (e.g., 16:10–18).[12]

Not only is Paul a teamworker, but his traveling ministry and mission is based on his relationship with the community in Antioch. It is they who, directed by the Holy Spirit, send him and Barnabas out (13:1–3), after this duo have served in what appears to be the leadership team of that community (13:1). It is to Antioch that Barnabas and Saul return after their travels and report back on what God has been doing through them (14:26–27), and they stay for some time with the community there (14:28) before being appointed by the Antioch community to go to Jerusalem in response to debate with the circumcision group (15:1–2). After the Jerusalem meeting, they return to Antioch (15:30), where they stay for "some days" (τινας ἡμέρας, *tinas hēmeras*, 15:36).

Examples of Communal Decision-Making

Not only did the early believers live and act communally, they also made their decisions that way. Let us consider some examples.

The Choice of Matthias 1:15–26

Here we meet the community at a time of transition. They are waiting, following the command of Jesus, for the coming of the Spirit, and as they wait they pray together in unity—notice again the stress on their shared life (v. 14).[13] The loss of Judas, who betrayed Jesus and subsequently died, requires attention, and Peter leads the community in reflecting and acting. Peter

---

11. Interestingly, Timothy is not named in Acts as part of that team (17:1, 4, 5, 10).

12. For a discussion of the possible meanings of the plurals, see Porter, "The 'We' Passages."

13. See discussion of the key term ὁμοθυμαδόν, *homothymadon*, in Walton, "Ὁμοθυμαδόν," 101.

reads Pss 68:26 LXX (MT 69:25) and 108:8 LXX (MT 109:8) as speaking of Judas's betrayal; both come from psalms of lament in a situation where a godly person suffers at the hand of ungodly people, and Ps 108 LXX was understood by early Christians to speak of Jesus's unjust suffering.[14] Here, Peter interprets them as applicable to Judas who is an ungodly man par excellence who betrayed Jesus into the hands of other ungodly people. The story of Judas's gruesome death (vv. 18–19) is laid alongside these verses (v. 20) to draw the conclusion that Judas must be replaced by another (vv. 21–22). The replacement will restore the number of twelve, a key development of the early community, because Luke stresses that Israel is being restored and renewed[15]—hence the need for twelve, to symbolize the twelve tribes.

Having laid the situation out and interpreted it by reading Scripture, Peter offers a person specification for the one they need (vv. 21–22), and the decision is placed in two sets of hands. First, the community—the 120 people (v. 15)—identify two men who could do the job: Barsabbas Justus and Matthias. Human assessment and work go into the appointment. Secondly, the final decision is placed into God's hands as they pray for wisdom (vv. 24–25) and cast lots (v. 26). Some think that the casting of lots was mistaken, and point to the lack of casting lots after Pentecost, when the Spirit has come upon the whole believing community—and even speculate that they should have waited, for Paul was the one who should have been the twelfth apostle.[16] That seems unlikely, however, given the stress on the restoration of Israel in the early chapters of Acts. Casting lots removes all human interference in the choice and places the decision in God's hands (Prov 16:33)—it was not understood as random in the way in which Westerners see it today, whether in Jewish or Greco-Roman society. Paul himself, of course, lacked the qualification of having been with Jesus from the beginning through to the resurrection, so he would not have been eligible in any case.[17]

This decision, in other words, is a combination of human and divine, and the human part is a corporate part—it is not the apostles, or Peter alone, who select the candidates, but "they," that is the community.

---

14. E.g., Matt 27:34, 48; Mark 15:23, 36; Luke 23:36; John 2:17; 15:25; 19:29; Rom 15:3.

15. Cf. 1:6–8; 3:21. See the fine discussion in Bauckham, "Restoration."

16. E.g., Stier, *Words*, 12–15.

17. Note 1 Cor 15:3–5, where it says that he received resurrection stories from others.

PART I: ENGAGING ETHICALLY WITHIN CHRISTIAN COMMUNITY

Rejecting the Sanhedrin's Requirement of Silence 4:23–31

As a second example, consider the community's response to the Sanhedrin's instruction to Peter and John that they should not speak further in the name of Jesus (4:18). Peter and John report back on what has happened (v. 23).[18] The group then engage with the situation in unity (ὁμοθυμαδόν, *homothymadon*, again, v. 24) and pray together—Luke portrays a united prayer in one voice, as "those who heard" address God. Their prayer builds on the promise of Jesus, that "you will be my witnesses" (1:8), and offers a reading of Ps 2:1–2 as a lens through which they interpret their present and recent experience (vv. 25–28). Shockingly, they identify the opponents of God in the psalm with the present Jewish leadership as well as the Romans, whereas in the psalm it is the pagan nations who oppose God's people (v. 27).

It is the *community* who call on God to "pay attention to their threats," using language that is used elsewhere for God's care for creation and for his people.[19] It has the force of the American idiom "take care of," which means "deal with"—such as, "Let me take care of that bill." They have come to a mind through reading Scripture together concerning what God's purpose is, and now they ask God to enable them to keep speaking[20] the message of Jesus boldly. As with the choice of Matthias, placing the situation into God's hands results in a divine response—the place is shaken (v. 31), after the manner of rushing wind at Pentecost (2:2), and the Spirit refills them so that they do speak boldly.

Choosing the Seven 6:1–7

As we noted earlier, the dispute over the care of widows in 6:1–7 is evidence of the nature of the shared life of the believers in Jerusalem, for the two language groups among the believers (Hellenists and Hebrews) must have been sufficiently involved with one another for them to know what was happening. It is striking that the Twelve's response is not to decide what to do by themselves, but instead to call a community meeting to resolve the situation (v. 2). Potentially, this is a massive group, since the believing community may

---

18. It is not completely clear whether τοὺς ἰδίους, *tous idious* (v. 23) indicates the apostolic band or the wider believing community; either way, the situation is presented to a group for response.

19. Job 22:12; Pss 34:17 (MT 35:17); 112:6; 137:6 (MT 138:6); 2 Macc 8:2.

20. This is the probable force of the present infinitive λαλεῖν, *lalein* (v. 29).

now be over five thousand (4:4), so the meeting would have needed to take place somewhere public, such as in the temple courts—there is no handling of their dirty washing in private for the early believers!

As with replacing Judas, the apostles offer leadership by proposing a solution, that the community chooses seven to oversee this matter. Notably, they use the same vocabulary for the role of the seven, "to *serve* tables" (διακονεῖν τραπέζαις, *diakonein trapezais*, v. 2), as they do for their own apostolic role, "the *service* of the word" (τῇ διακονίᾳ τοῦ λόγου, *tē diakonia tou logou*, v. 4), so this is not setting up a hierarchy of importance that would suggest that the apostles' work is more important than that of the seven—they are all "serving."

The community responds in two ways: by affirming the proposed solution, and by nominating seven candidates for the role of overseeing the provision for the widows (v. 5). At least one, Stephen, is from the Greek-speaking group whose widows are being neglected, for he engages with a Greek-speaking synagogue later on (6:8–10); others have Greek names and thus may be Hellenists too. The seven are then commissioned and prayed for in their role, and it is notable here that it is not simply the apostles who prayed and laid hands on them, in spite of what most English versions say. Rather, the Greek is most naturally read as portraying the whole group laying hands on and praying for the seven.[21] Thus the decision is made and executed by the community, a process that reflects the universal gift of the Spirit to the community (2:17, 38; cf. Num 11:29).

Again, we see God's hand in this event, for the summary in verse 7 makes clear that the community continues to grow as the word spreads, even among priests. God works with and through the decision-making of the community—well-fed widows would demonstrate the reality of the impact of the gospel and the gift of the Spirit among Jews, who would be horrified if needy people like widows were neglected.[22]

Welcoming Saul of Tarsus in Jerusalem 9:26–30

When Saul of Tarsus meets the exalted Jesus on the road to Damascus, he is welcomed by the believing community of Antioch as he immediately begins proclaiming this Jesus (9:19b–21). Presumably Ananias spoke of the reality of Saul's transformation from persecutor to believer, as Ananias himself had

---

21. See my forthcoming commentary in WBC, ad loc.
22. See the fine discussion in Biggar, "Showing."

heard the Lord speak about this and had been the one who baptized Saul and prayed for his healing from temporary blindness (9:10–18).

Things become trickier when Saul goes to Jerusalem for the first time since his encounter with Jesus, for the community there are, understandably, cautious of him (v. 26). Here Barnabas plays a key role, for he shares testimony with the apostles about the reality of Saul's faith and meeting with the Lord, and his preaching of Jesus in Damascus (v. 27). This is a fascinating case of testimony changing how a community thinks, and it is noteworthy that Barnabas's testimony is expressed from Saul's point of view (v. 27). The result is that the community accepts Saul as a genuine believer and supports him (vv. 28–29a), and then arranges for him to leave for safety in Tarsus when there is a threat to his life (v. 29b–30). The community's decision-making here is focused in the acceptance of Saul by the apostolic group on the basis of Barnabas's testimony. Further, yet again, God's action goes with community decision, for Saul not only speaks boldly in Jesus's name—a mark of the Spirit's work in him (v. 28; cf. 4:30–31)—but speaks with other Greek-speaking Jews about the Lord (v. 29a).

The Spirit Calling Barnabas and Saul from Antioch 13:1–3

We meet Saul with Barnabas again in (Syrian) Antioch, working among the believing community there. Barnabas brings Saul there to work with him among the first Jew–Gentile community (11:25–26), and they seem to have been there for some years by the time of the events in Acts 13. By then, they are part of a multicultural, multi-age, and multiethnic five-person leadership team (v. 1) in the community there. As the group[23] are worshipping the Lord and fasting, the Spirit speaks to them (v. 2), probably through one of those identified as a prophet (v. 1), for "the Holy Spirit said" is echoed in Agabus's words later (21:11).

The community then take their time in responding to this prophetic announcement. The wording "Then, after they fasted and prayed" (v. 3) suggests that a further time of fasting and praying took place before the decision was made that this was indeed the voice of the Spirit, and thus that they should send Barnabas and Saul out. It is not hard to see why such

---

23. It is not completely clear whether αὐτῶν, *autōn* (v. 1) refers to the five names in verse 1 or the wider Antioch community; either way, the experience which follows is a group experience and decision.

discernment was necessary, for the community was potentially losing two of its five key leaders, and they would want to be as sure as possible that this was God's purpose. Not only that, but we know from Paul's writings that the proper response to a prophet speaking was for the community to discern what was the voice of God from what the prophet said (e.g., 1 Cor 14:29; 1 Thess 5:20–21).[24] Prophecy here does not give infallible access to God's mind—it requires human engagement, and corporate engagement at that, to discern what God is saying.

Going to Macedonia 16:6–10

One of the most puzzling and interesting incidents in Acts is the decision to go to Macedonia from Asia in Acts 16. For the only time in the Greek Old or New Testaments, the Spirit "hinders" (κωλύω, *kōlyō*, v. 6), and thus acts negatively to prevent Paul and his companions going to certain places. Luke is not specific about the means by which the Spirit hinders them from preaching in Asia (v. 6) or entering Bithynia (v. 7), but he is explicit that the Spirit engages directly with them in this process. Perhaps this is a further example of prophecy at work.

A rare example of specific divine guidance follows in the vision that Paul has at night of the Macedonian man calling for help (v. 9).[25] The man is beseeching or exhorting them (παρακαλῶν, *parakalōn*), rather than giving a clear command (contrast 10:5–6, where Cornelius is instructed by the angel to send for Peter), although this verb is in some tension with the imperative "help!" (βοήθησον, *boētheson*). The one who appears to Paul is human, rather than a divine character or agent, by contrast with most visions in Luke-Acts, where God or the Lord is the speaker or the Spirit or an angel.[26] Nevertheless, this vision is critical to events and facilitates a significant plot transition.[27]

---

24. See the very helpful discussion, highlighting the role of human discernment in understanding what God says, in Miller, *Convinced*. On the role of discernment in relation to prophecy specifically, see Grudem, *Gift*, 74–79.

25. Some wonder how Paul knew that the man was Macedonian: the phrase "come to Macedonia" (διαβὰς εἰς Μακεδονίαν, *diabas eis Makedonian*, v. 9) seems a clear indication of this.

26. E.g. Acts 10:3; Luke 1:11.

27. Miller, *Convinced*, 98.

It is Paul and his companions who respond to the vision—another example of corporate discernment and decision-making. Luke makes this clear by shifting from third person singular "he saw" (εἶδεν, *eiden*, v. 10) to first person plural "we began seeking" (ἐζητήσαμεν, *ezētēsamen*, v. 10). Luke's explanation of the ground for the decision is given in the following causal participial clause "since we were convinced that God had called us to evangelise them" (συμβιβάζοντες ὅτι προσκέκληται ἡμᾶς ὁ θεὸς εὐαγγελίσασθαι αὐτούς, *sumbibazontes hoti proskeklētai hēmas ho theos euangelisasthai autous*). The participle is plural, indicating that the decision that this was God's call was made by the group, not by Paul alone. Interestingly, there is no specific mention of God speaking to them, by contrast with "the Holy Spirit said" (13:2) and "the Lord spoke to Paul in a vision" (18:9–10). The group have to interpret Paul's experience of the dream in order to discern the next step they must take.

It is worth noticing what happens next, for after such a remarkable experience, which stands out because it is unusual, the mission in Macedonia is somewhat "underwhelming."[28] Certainly there are positive results, for Lydia becomes a believer (16:13–15), but there are the problems with the girl with the Pythian spirit (16:16–18) that result in Paul and Silas finding themselves in prison (16:19–24). There is no specified divine action to free them, neither miracle nor escape, by contrast with Peter (12:3–11), and there is no mention of God or an angel causing the earthquake. Indeed, they do not take the opportunity the earthquake provides to escape from jail, but stay put (16:25–28). The jailer and his family come to faith in Jesus (16:29–34), but Paul and Silas have to leave Philippi (16:40).

None of these events necessarily means that Paul and his companions got their interpretation of Paul's vision wrong. Indeed, if they were right, that suggests that getting God's will right does not automatically mean that things will be successful; this story rather suggests the reverse, that if the guidance seems remarkable and (relatively) clear, that may mean that things are going to be difficult.

Key Factors Involved

Looking over these examples, we can see four factors involved in the decision-making processes, all of which are conducted corporately. All

---

28. Miller, *Convinced*, 107.

four are not involved in every story, but they occur sufficiently to see a consistent pattern.

First, the believers trust God and are dependent on God. This finds expression in various ways: casting lots; prayer for God to act; interpreting Scripture, heard as God's voice; divine speech by the Spirit and by God; and dreams and visions that convey God's purposes.

However, secondly, each of these "divine" activities requires interpretation—they are not self-explanatory, but need the believing community to reflect and study in order to discern God's purposes. That discernment happens as they engage together in considering how to respond. For sure, it involves turning to God, as the Antiochene church does in further fasting and prayer (13:3), but there is real human involvement in this process in collaboration with God.

Thirdly, testimony to what God is doing is important, whether telling the story of recent events to show why a decision needs taking (as Peter does before the choice of Matthias), or speaking on behalf of one who is regarded with suspicion (as Barnabas does for Saul in Jerusalem), or (as we shall see) telling the story of God's action in the beginnings of the mission to Gentiles.

Fourthly, human leadership has a role in offering a path forward to the community, but it is never carried out in a dictatorial or authoritarian manner. Even before the coming of the Spirit on the whole community at Pentecost, it is the group who nominate the two potential apostles from whom Matthias is chosen by lot (1:23) in response to a proposal by Peter (1:21–22). After Pentecost, there is a clear role for the apostles in shaping a response to circumstances, but it is never done in isolation from the community. Thus, in choosing the seven, the community gathers at the apostles' invitation (6:2), and responds to the apostles' proposal (6:3) by choosing the seven (6:5) and commissioning them (6:6). Similarly, Paul (as team leader) tells his companions about the vision he has received, and the group then draws conclusions about God's purposes (16:10).

As we turn now to our major case study, the path to the inclusion of Gentiles in the believing community, we shall see these features repeated with some fresh features and factors as they together discern what God is doing.

PART I: ENGAGING ETHICALLY WITHIN CHRISTIAN COMMUNITY

The Inclusion of Gentiles

The story of Acts moves gradually from insiders to Judaism becoming believers towards rank outsiders being included in the community. After Pentecost, the healing of the man with a congenital disability at the temple marks the inclusion of one whose disability would have excluded him from temple worship (3:1–10)—and that is why his first action on being healed is to run and jump praising God and to enter the temple (3:8–9). Philip, as part of the group driven out of Jerusalem because of the persecution after Stephen's death (8:1, 4), goes to the half-breed Samaritans whom the Jews consider to be heretics and outsiders, and Samaritans are included in the gospel community with the approval of the Spirit, who comes on the believing Samaritans at the prayer of Peter and John (8:5–25). A further step occurs when Philip meets the Ethiopian eunuch (8:26–40), a meeting arranged carefully through an angel directing Philip (8:26). The eunuch has a deeply ambiguous status and had desired to worship in Jerusalem (8:27), but almost certainly had not been able to do so because he was castrated.[29] Nevertheless, he is seeking God, as his reading of Isaiah and his questions demonstrate (8:30–34), and through Philip he is baptized (8:36, 38). If the eunuch was a Gentile, as seems most likely, Luke makes no major point about this—it is a later story that Luke presents as the turning point in God's present actions.

This turning point happens through a further "divine appointment," this time arranged at the behest of an angel on one side, and a vision accompanied by a voice on the other. This is the story of Peter's encounter with Cornelius and his household, an encounter that is told three times in Acts, which highlights its significance (10:1–48; 11:1–18; 15:7–11).[30]

Peter Going to Cornelius 10:1–48

The first telling of the story, in 10:1–48, is from an external narrator's perspective. The story focuses separately on Cornelius (vv. 1–8) and Peter (vv. 9–23) until they are together in Cornelius's house (vv. 24–48). As the story develops, we see the same combination that we have seen elsewhere, of divine action and human interpretation, and the human interpretation is a corporate process.

---

29. Deut 23:1; Jeremias, *Jerusalem*, 343–44.
30. See Witherup, "Cornelius."

The divine initiative is clear, for an angel appears to the godly centurion Cornelius and instructs him to send for Peter (vv. 3–6). The angel instructs Cornelius what to do, but this would nevertheless require Cornelius to reflect and decide that he was not crazy, but had heard a genuine divine instruction. As a centurion in the occupying Roman army, however sympathetic he was to Jewish beliefs, he would not wish to appear foolish and gullible. He sends a *group* to Peter—two servants and a soldier whom he knows to be "devout" (εὐσεβής, *eusebēs*, v. 8)—and briefs the group about what has happened, thus trusting them to discern and respond appropriately to what they encounter in Joppa.

Peter's experience is similarly dramatic, for three times he has the same baffling vision of animals on a sheet that he is told to "kill and eat" (v. 13). Good Jew that he is, he knows that he must discriminate among animals and can only eat those permitted by the torah (v. 14). At this point, Peter is simply puzzled (v. 17a), but his puzzlement will be resolved at a later point. He is told more directly by the Spirit to go with the visitors who are just arriving (vv. 19–20), and responds—and without that divine speech he surely would not have shown hospitality to pagans (v. 23).

When Peter travels to Caesarea to visit Cornelius, he takes a group with him from the community in Joppa (v. 23b). Finally, when he meets Cornelius, the penny drops and he understands the vision of the animals on the sheet—it is not about animals but about people. He is not to "call anyone impure or unclean" (v. 28) and he (perhaps a little disingenuously) tells Cornelius that he came "without objection." The scene broadens out as Peter and the believers from Joppa meet Cornelius's household, potentially quite a large group, and Cornelius tells his side of the story. Now we hear the encounter with the angel filtered through Cornelius (vv. 30–33), and this edited version adds Cornelius's conclusion that he and his household want to hear what "you have been instructed to say by the Lord" (v. 33). Cornelius thus draws a conclusion from his vision, and invites Peter to share that conclusion.

Peter recognizes and agrees with Cornelius's interpretation of his own vision, and draws his own, quite remarkable, further conclusion, that God will accept people from every nation who fear him (vv. 34–35). In terms of the story of Acts, we see here a discernment process going on between these two men that leads to Peter telling the gospel message in terms familiar from the earlier evangelistic speeches in Acts (vv. 35–43). At this point,

Peter is interrupted by the outpouring of the Holy Spirit on the household (v. 44), evidenced by the Gentiles speaking in tongues and praying to God (v. 46). The group who came with Peter are astonished, but they draw the conclusion from these phenomena that this is the Spirit (vv. 45–46; note γάρ, *gar*—"for," introducing the ground for their interpretation). In agreement with the group's assessment, Peter draws the further conclusion that these people should be baptized, since they are clearly marked by the Spirit as members of the community (v. 47).

As in other stories, the discernment process here is a corporate one, even including someone who, at the outset of the story, is not yet a believer. The story itself is as much about the conversion of Peter—the transformation of his mind-set—as the conversion of Cornelius and his household, for Peter grows in understanding as he engages in discernment with others: the group Cornelius sends, the believers who travel from Joppa with him, and with Cornelius himself as he gives testimony to Peter.

Debate and Discernment in Jerusalem 11:1–18

On his return to Jerusalem, Peter faces challenges from Jewish believers over his acceptance of hospitality from uncircumcised men (v. 3). The challenge is over shared meals, for a key distinctive behavior of Jewish people was to keep the food laws of the torah. This meant that they were very cautious about what they ate: there is evidence of kosher meat stalls in the Corinthian meat market.[31] Such specialist stalls and shops would ensure both that the meat had been killed and hung according to Jewish practice and that it could not have been polluted by being offered in idol temples. Hence, Jewish people did not eat with Gentiles, since the meat they would be offered in a Gentile home would almost certainly be both non-kosher and tainted with idolatry.

Now we hear the story again, but this time filtered through Peter. This time we hear little of what happened with Cornelius, even though Peter knows Cornelius's story—for to persuade his audience in Jerusalem, Peter must convince them that it is the God of Israel who sent him to Cornelius and who has now accepted Cornelius. So Peter's speech focuses on the vision, and the way his thinking has been transformed by God's action. His reference to Cornelius is not by name—he is simply "the man" (v. 12)—and he says very little of the angel's appearance to Cornelius, but only reports

---

31. Winter, *After*, 293–95.

(some of) what the angel said, with an added clause, indicating that Cornelius knew that he and his household "will be saved" through Peter's message (v. 14). Peter makes it clear that a devout group ("these six brothers," v. 12) accompanied him, thus invoking their testimony to what took place—this was the group, recall, who concluded that God had acted in accepting the Gentiles (10:45–46). Peter then tells the story of the Spirit's coming and interprets it through the promise of Jesus (v. 16; cf. 1:5), and blames God for what has happened: "who was I that I could hinder God?" (v. 17). This testimony tips the balance for the critics, and they (perhaps a little reluctantly) concede that "even" (καί, *kai*) the Gentiles have been given repentance and life by God (v. 18).

The corporate process is very significant here in persuading the skeptics in Jerusalem that the acceptance of these Gentiles is truly God's work. In response to their questions, themselves part of the corporate discernment process, it requires a number of contributions to swing the decision: Peter's testimony, the (implicit) testimony of the six brothers, and the *interpretation* of events as being the action of God because they resemble their own experience at Pentecost. The latter implies that at least some of the doubting group were members of the original one hundred and twenty. Peter does not simply dictate what happens, however eminent he is considered to be, and however much God has clearly worked in and through him in the past growth and development of the community: it requires a corporate engagement with what is going on to be confident in discerning what God is doing.

Sending Barnabas to Antioch from Jerusalem 11:19–26

Luke now picks up from the scattering of the believers through persecution from Acts 8, verses 1 and 4 to explain what happens. Thus, it is likely that these events are happening around the same time as Peter's visit to Cornelius: the gradual inclusion of Gentiles in the believing community is not entirely dependent on one event.

The thing to notice here is that the scattered believers arrive in Syrian Antioch and start to talk "also to Greeks" (v. 20)—not Greek-speaking Jews, as in Jerusalem (6:1), but outright Gentiles.[32] The result is that a substantial

---

32. The word used is Ἑλληνιστής, *Hellēnistēs* in both 6:1 (where it is clearly speaking about Greek-speaking Jews) and 11:20 (where the contrast with μόνον Ἰουδαίοις,

PART I: ENGAGING ETHICALLY WITHIN CHRISTIAN COMMUNITY

number of Gentiles become believers (v. 21), and this raises a similar issue to the conversion of Cornelius: is this a genuine work of God?

The Jerusalem community's response to this news is to reflect, and to send Barnabas as a delegate to see what is going on (v. 22). Barnabas goes, not on his own initiative, but to advise the community in Jerusalem, which is still led by the apostles (note 8:1)—we might think of Jerusalem as functioning at this point as a "mother church." The outcome is that Barnabas recognizes that God is at work in his grace, and then takes the initiative to fetch Saul from Tarsus—he knows Saul from his earlier visit to Jerusalem (9:26-30)—and he and Saul teach the church in Antioch (vv. 25-26).

The decision-making about this new step of speaking to Greeks about Jesus is again a corporate process. The community in Jerusalem takes responsibility for assessing what is happening and sends Barnabas as their representative to investigate. They clearly trust Barnabas's judgment of the new situation—and that trust is vindicated as the community in Antioch grows to the point where they can send financial help to the Jerusalem believers during a famine (11:27-30).

The Jerusalem Meeting 15:1-35

The drawing in of Gentiles continues through Barnabas and Saul's mission, initiated, as we saw, by the Spirit speaking to the community gathering in Antioch (13:1-3). Barnabas and Saul develop a pattern that will be the pattern of Paul's own ministry in later days: their first port of call in a new place is the Jewish synagogues (13:5), but they are also ready and willing to speak about Jesus with Gentiles when opportunities arise, as they do on Cyprus when the proconsul Sergius Paulus summons Paul to speak with him (13:7-12). More than that, when the synagogue community is divided—as frequently happens—they deliberately go to Gentiles and speak of Jesus. This is their experience in Pisidian Antioch (13:14-52). The proclamation of Jesus divides the synagogue, particularly because word spreads in the city and many Gentiles come to hear Paul speak (13:44-45), and this provokes a zealous anti-Gentile reaction among some of the Jews. At this point Paul and Barnabas make what can be misunderstood to be an absolute change of direction, towards Gentiles and away from Jews (13:46),

---

monon Ioudaiois, "only to Jews" in v. 19 makes it clear that non-Jewish Greek speakers are intended).

and they interpret present events through the lens of Scripture in making this decision, quoting Isa 49:6 (13:47). However, it is not an absolute change of direction, for when Paul and Barnabas arrive in Iconium, the next city they visit, the first place that they go to is the synagogue (14:1), with similar results to Antioch—the Jewish community is divided; some join Paul and Barnabas, and others revile them and plot to stone them to death (14:2–5). This pattern continues as Paul and Barnabas travel through Phrygia and southern Galatia, and they eventually return to Syrian Antioch, their "sending church," and report "all that God had done, and that he had opened a door of faith to the Gentiles" (14:27).

However, not all the believers are happy about this development, and the issue that appeared in 11:1 after Peter's visit to Cornelius returns—on what basis can Gentiles be members of the believing communities? I think it is likely that Paul writes Galatians around this time,[33] as he hears of the issue and responds in this most polemical letter to clarify his view, that Gentiles do not need to be circumcised and keep the law in order to be believers—exactly the same issue that is raised in Acts 15:1. Paul and Barnabas engage in debate with the Judean Jewish believers who want Gentile believers to be circumcised and keep the law, and the result is that the Antiochene community sends them as delegates to discuss with the Jerusalem apostles and elders what to do (15:2b–4). Here we see the most critical decision that the early believers face. It is not about whether Gentiles can be accepted by God—all Jews believed that was possible already, providing they took the yoke of the law and were circumcised (if men) or went through a ritual bath (if women). The debate was about whether Gentile believers had to take the yoke of the law to be followers of Jesus, or whether God accepted them without that commitment, and thus whether Jewish and Gentile believers could be recognized as part of one community of God's people purely on the basis of faith in Jesus.

The meeting in Jerusalem was an extended affair: there had been "much debate" (15:7) before Peter stood to speak. Peter's speech is strongly focused on God and what God is doing, echoing and alluding to his experience with Cornelius: almost all the main verbs have God as subject, and the critical question is, "Why are you trying to test God?" (v. 10). This chimes in with the testimony that Paul and Barnabas had given on their arrival in

---

33. The issue is debated; the clinching argument is that, had the Jerusalem meeting happened before Paul wrote Galatians, why would Paul not cite the ruling from the apostles and elders in Jerusalem? For discussion of the issues involved, see Longenecker, *Galatians*, lxxii–lxxxiii.

the city of "all that God had done with them" (v. 4), a testimony that is now repeated in the larger gathering (v. 12).

James—probably the brother of Jesus—exercises a role of leadership by proposing a solution to the gathering. He interprets contemporary events through Scripture, drawing particularly on Amos 9:11–12 (and snippets of other OT passages).[34] He sees the restoration of Israel through the founding and growth of the believing community as so far in train that Amos's expectation that the "tent of David" would be rebuilt has been fulfilled. This means, according to Amos, that the time has come in which Gentiles may "seek the Lord" (v. 17)—a common eschatological expectation among Second Temple Jews.[35] The surprising thing was that this means the age to come *has already arrived* in and through the life, death, resurrection, and exaltation of Jesus and the giving of the Spirit. James interprets events with this passage of Scripture to mean that it is not necessary for such Gentiles to undergo circumcision and to keep the law (v. 19). He is emphatic about this being his own view of the situation: "*I myself* (ἐγώ, *egō*) judge."

James's proposal, and its relationship to the text of the letter, is much debated in scholarship, and we do not have the space to discuss the various understandings of it here[36]—the key thing to notice for our purpose is that James does not make a ruling; he makes a proposal as to what "we" should do (vv. 19, 20). The apostles' and elders' response is to endorse and embrace this proposal: "it has seemed good to the Holy Spirit and to us" (v. 28) they write to the Gentile communities who sought their advice through Paul and Barnabas. Not only that, but the "whole assembly" (ὅλη τῇ ἐκκλησίᾳ, *holē tē ekklēsia*, v. 22) agrees to send delegates to share the decision with them, and they stress in the letter that they send with these delegates their unity in deciding to act in this way (ὁμοθυμαδόν, *homothymadon*, v. 25). Notice that this must mean that those who initially argued that Gentile believers must keep the law and be circumcised must have agreed with this decision, a remarkable change of view. Luke describes no steamrollering of those who disagreed—the process was sufficiently careful that a wide range of contributions were heard (we have only three reported in Luke's account); notice again that they debated for a long time (v. 7).

---

34. See valuable discussion in Bauckham, "James and the Jerusalem Church," esp. 453–58; Bauckham, "James and the Gentiles," esp. 155–70.

35. For the range of views, see the helpful discussion in Fuller, *Restoration*, 102–6.

36. Helpful discussion in Bauckham, "James and the Jerusalem Church," 460–67.

This was a critical moment in the life of the earliest believers, for it decided whether the believing communities were to continue to be an exclusive or inclusive community, whether they were (in effect) to be a new party within Judaism alongside others, such as the Sadducees, Pharisees, and Essenes, or were to embrace the purpose of God that through Abraham's descendants all the children of the earth would be blessed (Gen 12:1–3).

Lessons from This Process

In conclusion, let us sketch some features of this decision-making process that are striking and that have implications for how churches today make their decisions.

First, and perhaps most important of all, there is a focus on God that is combined with a real openness towards him. Instead of deciding in advance what God wants, they enter into conversation knowing what they presently think, but willing to engage fully with those with whom they disagree. They look for God's activity and actions in the stories they hear, and seek to discern God's purposes.

Secondly, they read contemporary events through the lens of Scripture, and interpret Scripture in the light of the remarkable events of the coming of Jesus, his death, resurrection, and exaltation, and the coming of the Spirit. We saw the believers doing this in reading Ps 2:1–2 when they prayed in response to the Sanhedrin's instruction to stop speaking in Jesus's name (4:24–30). We saw James drawing on Amos 9:11–12 in assessing the terms on which Gentiles were to be included in the community (15:13–18). This does not seem an arbitrary approach to Scripture that finds individual phrases or clauses that support a point irrespective of their context, but an in-depth engagement with Scripture's overall flow and a careful reading of texts in context. As C. H. Dodd taught us, so often when the NT authors cite a snippet or a verse of Scripture, we need to look at the whole context in the OT to hear the full message that is being invoked in the NT.[37]

Thirdly, they are ready to listen to testimony and to weigh that testimony in the light of Scripture and the purposes of God revealed there. The Jerusalem Jewish believers listen with care to Peter and draw the conclusion that God really has—to their surprise—accepted the Gentile Cornelius and his household (11:18). The apostles and elders listen to Paul and Barnabas speaking about their experience of Gentiles coming to faith (15:12), and

---

37. Dodd, *Scriptures*, passim, with a useful summary on 126–27.

also to Peter, who combines testimony with a focus on God (15:7–11)—"all that God had done" is a theme phrase for this whole process (14:27; 15:4, 12; cf. Luke 8:39).

Fourthly and finally, the process is corporate, open, and unhurried. The sequence of passages we have studied probably covers a period of some years, and the Jerusalem meeting itself was lengthy—long enough for different voices to be heard, and long enough for real reflection and change of mind to take place. The process was not held in secret: for sure, there was a clear role for leaders in the meeting, and for James in particular in proposing a solution to the presenting issue; but the decision was not settled in smoke-filled rooms with only a select group present and others excluded—as well as being corporate, there was (as we would now say) real transparency about the decision-making process.

Bibliography

Aitkenhead, Decca. "Rachel Dolezal: 'I'm Not Going to Stoop and Apologise and Grovel.'" *The Guardian* (February 25, 2017). https://www.theguardian.com/us-news/2017/feb/25/rachel-dolezal-not-going-stoop-apologise-grovel.

Bauckham, Richard. "James and the Gentiles (Acts 15.13–21)." In *History, Literature, and Society in the Book of Acts*, edited by Ben Witherington III, 154–84. Cambridge: Cambridge University Press, 1996.

———. "James and the Jerusalem Church." In *The Book of Acts in its Palestinian Setting*, edited by Richard Bauckham, 415–80. BAFCS 4. Grand Rapids: Eerdmans, 1995.

———. "The Restoration of Israel in Luke-Acts." In *Restoration: Old Testament, Jewish and Christian Perspectives*, edited by James M. Scott, 435–87. JSJSup 72. Leiden: Brill, 2001.

Biggar, Nigel. "Showing the Gospel in Social Praxis." *Anvil* 8, no. 1 (1991) 7–18.

Dodd, C. H. *According to the Scriptures: The Sub-structure of New Testament Theology*. London: Nisbet, 1952.

Ellis, E. E. "Coworkers, Paul and His." In *Dictionary of Paul and the Letters*, edited by Gerald F. Hawthorne et al., 183–89. Downers Grove: IVP, 1993.

Frizell, Sam. "Rachel Dolezal: I Was Born White." *Time* (November 3, 2015). http://time.com/4096959/rachel-dolezal-white/.

Fuller, Michael E. *The Restoration of Israel: Israel's Re-gathering and the Fate of the Nations in Early Jewish Literature and Luke-Acts*. BZNW 138. Berlin: de Gruyter, 2006.

Gregson, Fiona J. Robertson. *Everything in Common? The Theology and Practice of the Sharing of Possessions in Community in the New Testament*. Eugene, OR: Pickwick, 2017.

Grudem, Wayne A. *The Gift of Prophecy in the New Testament and Today*. Eastbourne: Kingsway, 1988.

Jeremias, Joachim. *Jerusalem in the Time of Jesus* [*Jerusalem zur Zeit Jesu*]. London: SCM, 1969.

Longenecker, Richard N. *Galatians*. WBC 41. Dallas, TX: Word, 1990.

Lyman, Eric J. "Latin Mass Resurgent 50 Years after Vatican II." *USA Today* (March 13, 2015). https://eu.usatoday.com/story/news/world/2015/03/12/catholicism-latin-mass-resurgence/70214976/.

Miller, John B. F. *Convinced That God Had Called Us: Dreams, Visions, and the Perception of God's Will in Luke-Acts*. BibInt 85. Leiden: Brill, 2007.

Mosendz, Polly. "Family Accuses NAACP Leader Rachel Dolezal of Falsely Portraying Herself as Black." *Newsweek* (June 12, 2015). http://www.newsweek.com/family-accuses-naacp-leader-rachel-dolezal-falsely-portraying-herself-black-342511.

Porter, Stanley E. "The 'We' Passages." In *The Book of Acts in Its Graeco-Roman Setting*, edited by David W. J. Gill and Conrad H. Gempf. BAFCS 2, 545–74. Grand Rapids: Eerdmans, 1994.

Stier, Rudolf. *The Words of the Apostles*. 2nd ed. Edinburgh: T. & T. Clark, 1869.

Walton, Steve. "Primitive Communism in Acts? Does Acts Present the Community of Goods (2:44–45; 4:32–35) as Mistaken?" *Evangelical Quarterly* 80, no. 2 (2008) 99–111.

———. "'Ομοθυμαδόν in Acts: Co-location, Common Action or 'Of One Heart and Mind'?" In *The New Testament in its First Century Setting: Essays on Context and Background in Honour of B. W. Winter on His 65th Birthday*, edited by P. J. Williams et al., 89–105. Grand Rapids: Eerdmans, 2004.

Winter, Bruce W. *After Paul Left Corinth: The Influence of Secular Ethics and Social Change*. Grand Rapids: Eerdmans, 2001.

Witherup, Ronald D., SS. "Cornelius Over and Over and Over Again: 'Functional Redundancy' in the Acts of the Apostles." *JSNT* 49 (1993) 45–66.

3

Jonathan Edwards on Contemplating the Beautiful God

Some Pastoral Reflections

MICHAEL BRÄUTIGAM[1]

MANY TODAY ASSOCIATE JONATHAN Edwards (1703–58) with his famous sermon "Sinners in the Hands of an Angry God." Edwards, so goes the common stereotype, was a passionate hellfire preacher. Yet this is not the whole story. While it is true that Edwards preached about the horrors of

---

1. I am grateful to Rhys Bezzant for helpful comments on an earlier draft of this chapter. I have also benefited from stimulating conversations with Douglas McComiskey and Thomas Kimber about its content. I presented an earlier version of this essay at the 2016 Jonathan Edwards for the Church conference in Durham, UK. In my reading of Jonathan Edwards, I am relying heavily on the excellent work of Oliver D. Crisp and Kyle C. Strobel. See especially their recent collaboration, *Jonathan Edwards: An Introduction to His Thought*. John Bombaro has produced a stimulating treatment of Edwards's view on beauty in his *Jonathan Edwards's Vision of Reality* (see especially pp. 37–52 and 53–65). Relevant in this context is also Kin Yip Louie's contribution, *The Beauty of the Triune God*. Owen Strachan and Douglas A. Sweeney have put forward a highly readable booklet entitled, *Jonathan Edwards on Beauty*. Sang Hyun Lee's exploration of "Edwards and Beauty" is a very helpful one (pp. 113–25). Dane C. Ortlund has written a very accessible work on Edwards's understanding of beauty: *Edwards on the Christian Life* (ch. 1 is especially relevant for our purposes). Several of Edwards's key references to the idea of beauty mentioned in the works of these authors have found their way into this chapter. All Scripture quotations, unless otherwise indicated, are taken from the ESV.

hell—as did many of his contemporaries—he also highlighted the beauty of heaven. In fact, "Edwards was not obsessed by the wrath of God, but by his beauty," John Bombaro notes.[2] The very idea of beauty is central to Jonathan Edwards's theology.[3] "[W]e are concerned with nothing else," he writes.[4] If one seeks to arrive at a more balanced picture of Edwards, it is promising to take a closer look at his idea of beauty, which lies at the heart of his theological enterprise. My goal in this chapter is twofold: I first offer some general observations regarding the prominent place of beauty in Edwards's theology. In a second step I will draw out the implications for our Christian life and experience. The focus therefore moves from theological reflections on the nature of beauty to more experiential questions. More precisely, I intend to examine, first, Edwards's idea of the beauty of creation as it reflects the beautiful Creator. From this we move on to discuss, secondly, Edwards's foundational observations on the beautiful God, as the members of the Godhead relate to each other in mutual love and consent. Particularly important for Edwards in this context is the beautiful Jesus Christ who demonstrates a harmonious union of will with the Father. Having established the theological foundation of Edwards's idea of beauty, we are, thirdly, in the position to draw significant implications for our Christian life and experience. How does our experience of Christ's beauty affect us, perhaps even transform us? In my view, we would do well in rediscovering the important spiritual practice of contemplation in this regard. According to Edwards, contemplating the beautiful Christ is not only a joyful activity that incidentally reflects the Father's gaze upon his own Son, but it also leads to a significant character transformation.[5]

The Beauty of Creation Reflects the Beautiful Creator

First of all, Jonathan Edwards perceived the beauty of God's creation with eyes wide open. He marveled at the beautiful objects that stimulated the

---

2. Bombaro, *Jonathan Edwards's Vision*, 14.

3. See Delattre, *Beauty and Sensibility*, 1–2; Mitchell, *Experience of Beauty*; Crisp and Strobel, *Jonathan Edwards: An Introduction*, 58–66.

4. Edwards, *WJE*, 6:332. Jonathan Edwards's "placement of beauty at the heart of his theology," write McClymond and McDermott, "may have been the boldest stroke of all." McClymond and McDermott, *Theology of Jonathan Edwards*, 94.

5. Crisp and Strobel, *Jonathan Edwards: An Introduction*, 40.

receptors of his retinae: "We admire at the beauty of creation, at the beautiful order of it," he writes, "at the glory of the sun, moon, and stars."[6] Edwards not only delighted in astronomical bodies far away, but also, closer to home, in the beautiful rainbow,[7] and, even more close-up, he acquired a liking for creepy crawlies. With much enthusiasm he described his observations of the spider's "abundance of pleasure" as it was "sailing in the air."[8] It remains to be seen whether Edwards, had he lived in Australia as I do now, would have spoken with similar excitement at the sight of a full-grown Huntsman spider. There are, at least, grounds for reasonable doubt. "Abundance of horror" seems, in my view, a more appropriate remark when faced with an unfortunate arachnoid encounter such as this. Spiders aside, we note Edwards's aesthetic delight in the intricacies of God's creation, in its harmony, symmetry, and proportion. Edwards now establishes a direct link between the beauty of creation and the beautiful Creator. The beautiful things we perceive in the visible universe are in fact reflections of true beauty, namely God's perfect beauty. "[A]ll the beauty to be found throughout the whole creation," he writes, "is but the reflection of the diffused beams of that Being who hath an infinite fullness of brightness and glory."[9] Edwards makes clear that God is "the foundation and fountain" of all that is beautiful.

> God is not only infinitely greater and more excellent than all other being, but he is the head of the universal system of existence; the foundation and fountain of all being and all beauty; from whom all is perfectly derived, and on whom all is most absolutely and perfectly dependent; *of whom*, and *through whom*, and *to whom* is all being and all perfection; and whose being and beauty is as it were the sum and comprehension of all existence and excellence: much more than the sun is the fountain and summary comprehension of all the light and brightness of the day.[10]

---

6. Edwards, *WJE*, 10:420.

7. See Edwards, *WJE*, 6:298–301.

8. Edwards, *WJE*, 6:164.

9. Edwards, *WJE*, 8:550–51. Bombaro writes: "God's beauty is, as it were, the beautiful landscape out of which the flower of creation emerges." Bombaro, *Jonathan Edwards's Vision*, 63. For a discussion of Edwards's panentheist tendencies, see Bombaro, 297–99; see also Crisp, "Jonathan Edwards' Panentheism," 107–26. For a more recent resistance regarding the panentheist reading of Edwards, see Crisp and Strobel, *Jonathan Edwards: An Introduction*, 94–106.

10. Edwards, *WJE*, 8:551 (emphasis original).

From this vantage point, one recognizes clearly that for Edwards, the beauty of the natural world (what he also calls secondary beauty), pales in comparison to God's (primary) beauty.[11] Everything we see with our physical eyes, beautiful as it might be, is simply "deformity and darkness in comparison of the brighter glories and beauties of the Creator of all."[12] So yes, creation is beautiful, it is carefully handcrafted by God—it even emerges from the very beauty of God—but the beautiful God himself is unparalleled, above and beyond everything we find around us. "God's beauty is infinitely more valuable than that of all other beings," writes Edwards.[13] In fact, it is God's very beauty that distinguishes him from us, that makes him the wholly other God. "God is God, and distinguished from all other beings, and exalted above 'em, chiefly by his divine beauty, which is infinitely diverse from all other beauty."[14] Yet in what exactly does God's beauty exist? In which sense can we speak of God as the beautiful God par excellence? We should point out, first of all, that Edwards understands beauty as an ontological category. "Many considerations shape Edwards's ontology," writes Roland Delattre, "but none is more decisive than his concept of beauty."[15] Beauty, in Edwards's view, is the fundamental characteristic of being. Beauty is not an attribute that we could ascribe to God, or dissect and isolate from his being, but it is something that God *is*, that defines him exhaustively. Beauty, writes Edwards, is "that . . . wherein divinity chiefly consists."[16] The "category of beauty [is] . . . fundamental for Edwards's doctrine of God."[17] Still, we wonder, what exactly does Edwards mean when he speaks of the God-who-is-beauty? Edwards's train of thought takes us right into the realm of the intimate and harmonious interrelations of the holy Trinity, of Father, Son, and Holy Spirit. As we shall explore next, Edwards ultimately arrives at a definition of beauty that is distinctly relational, marked by love and consent.

---

11. Edwards, *WJE*, 6:336; 8:561–74; see Crisp and Strobel, *Jonathan Edwards: An Introduction* (58–66) for a discussion of primary and secondary beauty.
12. Edwards, *WJE*, 10:421.
13. Edwards, *WJE*, 8:551.
14. Edwards, *WJE*, 2:298.
15. Delattre, *Beauty and Sensibility*, 29.
16. Edwards, *WJE*, 2:298.
17. Crisp and Strobel, *Jonathan Edwards: An Introduction*, 58.

PART I: ENGAGING ETHICALLY WITHIN CHRISTIAN COMMUNITY

The Beautiful Trinity: Plurality, Love, and Consent

Edwards suggests that God is beautiful since the three persons of the Godhead enjoy glorious relationships of love and consent. Plurality, love, and consent are the three main building blocks of Edwards's idea of the beautiful God.[18] First, with a view to plurality, Edwards claims: "[W]e have shown that one alone cannot be excellent.... Therefore, if God is excellent, there must be a plurality in God."[19] Edwards uses the term "excellent," by the way, as a synonym for beauty.[20] Plurality in God is the foundation for harmonious relationship and this is what makes God truly beautiful. "All beauty," Edwards states, "consists in similarity or identity of relations."[21] And the highest expression of beauty is found in the most exquisite of all relationships, namely the eternal fellowship between Father, Son, and Holy Spirit. Here do we see the full expression of spiritual, or primary beauty.[22] On this basis, writes Kin Yip Louie, "Edwards is able to develop a relational ontology in which God's beauty is defined in terms of relationships."[23] For God to be, is to be in relation, and this is inherently beautiful.[24] Second, the beautiful inter-Trinitarian relationships are characterized by *love* for and *delight in* the other person. Edwards writes:

> As to God's excellence, it is evident it consists in the love of himself.... [H]e exerts himself towards himself no other way than in infinitely loving and delighting in himself, in the mutual love of the Father and the Son. This makes the third, the personal Holy Spirit, of the holiness of God, which is his infinite beauty, and this is God's infinite consent to being in general.[25]

According to Edwards, God is beautiful in that the Father loves his Son with a perfect love, a love that is in fact the Holy Spirit, and the Father is loved in

18. See Platinga Pauw, "The Trinity," 51–57.
19. Edwards, *WJE*, 13:284.
20. See McClymond and McDermott, *Theology of Jonathan Edwards*, 97.
21. Edwards, *WJE*, 6:334.
22. In Edwards's view, "God's beauty is the highest form of primary beauty or loving consent and consists of the most complex form of relationality, which as a whole makes up the highest form of proportion." Lee, "Edwards and Beauty," 114.
23. Louie, *Beauty of the Triune God*, 99.
24. Lee, *Philosophical Theology*, 77–80.
25. Edwards, *WJE*, 6:364.

return by the Son.[26] "[A]n infinitely holy and sweet energy arises between the Father and the Son," Edwards writes, "for their love and joy is mutual, in mutually loving and delighting in each other."[27] For Edwards, the relationship of love between Father and Son through the Spirit, Kyle Strobel notes, "is the archetype of beauty itself."[28] In our attempt to find answers to the question, "What makes God beautiful?," we have made considerable progress. The persons of the Trinity are beautiful because they relate to each other in love, a love that is characterized by mutual affection, harmony, and joy. Now Edwards is keen to add one more element to his definition of divine beauty. For Edwards, the key to what makes the loving relationship between the persons of the Trinity beautiful is that there exists between them a perfect union of will that he calls "agreement" or "consent."[29] Edwards intentionally chooses the language of volition when referring to beauty: "This is an universal definition of excellency: The consent of being to being, or being's consent to entity. The more the consent is, and the more extensive, the greater is the excellency."[30] What Edwards sees in the Trinitarian relationships is perfect understanding, a perfect harmony of will, and this is for Edwards central to what makes God beautiful. God is beautiful in that the members of the Godhead harmoniously relate towards each other in voluntary embrace. Within the Trinity there is neither conflict nor controversy. Father and Son embrace and affirm each other through the Spirit and they are harmoniously united in their willing with one another through the Holy Spirit.[31] They want the same, they have the same aspirations and inclinations, and they pursue the same goals. Consent within the Trinity is most profoundly demonstrated in the second person's consent to humble himself, to assume a human nature, and

---

26. "God hath respect to this man and loveth him as his own Son; this man hath communion with the Logos, in the love which the Father hath to him as his only begotten Son. Now the love of God is the Holy Ghost." Edwards, "Miscellanies 487," *WJE*, 13:529.

27. Edwards, *WJE*, 21:121.

28. Strobel, "The Beauty of Christ," 101.

29. Edwards writes: "One alone, without any reference to any more, cannot be excellent; for in such case there can be no manner of relation no way, and therefore, no such thing as consent. Indeed, what we call 'one' may be excellent, because of a consent of parts, or some consent of those in that being that are distinguished into a plurality some way or other. But in a being that is absolutely without any plurality there cannot be excellency, for there can be no such thing as consent or agreement." Edwards, *WJE*, 6:337.

30. Edwards, *WJE*, 6:336.

31. See Edwards, *WJE*, 21:121.

to atone for our sins.³² Edwards's rather speculative philosophical language is clearly rooted in Scripture: one thinks of the apostle Paul's language here, as he speaks of Christ Jesus, "who, though he was in the form of God, did not count equality with God a thing to be grasped, but emptied himself, by taking the form of a servant, being born in the likeness of men" (Phil 2:6–7).

Jesus Christ is beautiful (or, excellent) in Edwards's eyes since he humbled himself and freely agreed to the Father's plan of salvation, even though it would come at a great cost. "In the eternal covenant of redemption, the Son covenants with the Father to give himself to his people in love."³³ In the person of Christ divinity and humanity are harmoniously united through the Holy Spirit. This marvelous unity of humility and glory is what makes the person of Christ uniquely beautiful. Edwards explains:

> In the person of Christ do meet together, infinite glory, and the lowest humility. Infinite glory, and the virtue of humility, meet in no other person but Christ. They meet in no created person; for no created person has infinite glory: and they meet in no other divine person but Christ. For though the divine nature be infinitely abhorrent to pride, yet humility is not properly predictable of God the Father, and the Holy Ghost, that exist only in the divine nature; because it is a proper excellency only of a created nature. . . . But in Jesus Christ, who is both God and man, these two diverse excellencies, are sweetly united. He is a person infinitely exalted in glory and dignity.³⁴

Filled with the Holy Spirit (who is divine beauty, in Edwards's view), Jesus Christ is beautiful on account of the "sweet unity" of divinity and humanity in him.³⁵ The person of Christ is beautiful and so is his work. Jesus's life and ministry display perfect obedience to the Father. He willingly submits to the authority of his Father and glorifies him through words and deeds. Jesus's willingness to embrace the cross, though, represents the ultimate demonstration of consent, and therefore, beauty. "Christ never did anything whereby his love to the Father was so eminently manifested," Edwards writes, "as in laying down his life, under such inexpressible sufferings, in obedience to his command, and for the

32. For Edwards's views on the atonement, see Crisp and Strobel, *Jonathan Edwards: An Introduction*, 121–45.

33. Crisp and Strobel, *Jonathan Edwards: An Introduction*, 123.

34. Edwards, *WJE*, 19:567–68.

35. See Delattre, *Beauty and Sensibility*, 156–57; Crisp and Strobel, *Jonathan Edwards: An Introduction*, 58–66.

vindication of the honor of his authority and majesty."[36] It is certainly no coincidence that Edwards links here in this statement volition (obedience) with honour and majesty—or, we could say, beauty. Jesus is beautiful, as he displays perfect union of will with the Father, agreeing to go all the way to the cross, "Not my will, but yours, be done" (Luke 22:42). For this reason, Edwards can see beauty even in the horrific events of the cross: he sees beauty in the way the Son voluntarily submits himself to the authority and will of the Father to redeem humankind.[37] "Father, the hour has come; glorify your Son that the Son may glorify you" (John 17:1). On the cross, Jesus reveals himself as the truly beautiful One who glorifies the Father perfectly.[38] Having surveyed, very briefly, the basic building blocks of Edwards's theology of beauty, we are now in the position to apply these insights to our Christian life and experience.

Contemplating the Beautiful God

Since the whole spectrum of our human experience is somewhat infused by God's beauty, we are invited not only to enjoy the various objects of nature or relationships for their own sake, but to recognize God's fingerprint in them and to turn in worship and praise to him. For Edwards, William M. Schweitzer claims, "all of reality is the harmonious communication of the Triune divine mind."[39] Orchids, pine trees, dogs, Rilke's poems, and Rodin's Kiss, or a shared meal with friends, all provide us with an occasion to rejoice in our glorious creator God. In order to see God's fingerprint in creation, though, we need special divine intervention. What is required is nothing less than a new sense that comes only through divine intervention. With this new sense, the believer now "sees the wonderfulness of God's designs and a harmony

---

36. Edwards, *WJE*, 19:577.

37. In this context, I agree with Stephen Holmes who suggests that the idea of relation is central to Edwards's theology of atonement. The "key point" of Edwards's atonement theology, Holmes writes, "is that it is no abstract 'Justice' or even 'Goodness' that must be satisfied, but that, for Edwards, what goes on in the life, death and resurrection of Christ must make sense as a relational event between Christ, His Father, and the elect." For Holmes, "a personal/relational rationality underlies the [Edwards's] Christian doctrine of the atonement." See Holmes, *God of Grace*, 144–47.

38. "For Edwards, the cross, as with all things," write Owen Strachan and Doug Sweeney, "found its highest significance in relation to its glorification of God." Strachan and Sweeney, *Jonathan Edwards on Beauty*, 91.

39. Schweitzer, *God is a Communicative Being*, 6.

in all his ways, a harmony, excellency and wondrousness in his Word: he sees these things by an eye of faith, and by a new light that was never before let into his mind."[40] Edwards calls this new faculty in us a "new sense of the heart" through which we are able to taste and see things with new eyes—or, as Edwards put it, with new taste buds:

> Thus it is not he that has heard a long description of the sweetness of honey that can be said to have the greatest understanding of it, but he that has tasted ... The spiritual illumination of the minds of believers is resembled to tasting.[41]

This new sense of "tasting" and "seeing," though, needs to be consciously employed with devotion and care. It does not happen "automatically" as it were. This brings us to the important spiritual practice of contemplation. The idea of contemplation is easily misunderstood and thus calls for a careful definition. In recent times, contemplation has been treated with growing suspicion in some conservative evangelical circles.[42] It is feared that contemplation is simply about ecstatic spiritual-ethereal experiences detached from Scripture and propositional doctrinal statements. This concern is usually directed against some streams of mysticism in the Roman Catholic tradition. Conversely, voices in the Roman Catholic tradition have charged Protestants for their neglect of contemplation in favor of dogmatics. Hans Urs von Balthasar, for instance, while commending Protestantism's "vivid sense of Revelation in the Word," complains that it "often lacks something which would allow the study of the word of God to develop into true contemplation and vision."[43] In my view, evangelicals would do well to complement their doctrinal commitment with a distinct emphasis on contemplation. I thus welcome Carl Trueman's and Tom Schwanda's recent attempts to "retrieve" the practice of contemplation for evangelicals today.[44] In my view, there is much to learn from Edwards, who manages to hold in balance Scripture-based theology and deep contemplation of the divine things. What is contemplation? And how does contemplation differ from meditation? Based on Edwards's own thoughts,

40. Edwards, *WJE*, 14:79.

41. Edwards, *WJE*, 14:76.

42. See Schwanda, "Beauty of the Lord," 62–67. Thanks to Tom Kimber for pointing out this resource to me.

43. Balthasar, *Prayer*, 23.

44. Trueman, "Thoughtful Evangelicals," 2–4; Schwanda, "Beauty of the Lord," 62–84.

Kyle Strobel offers some helpful answers here.[45] Whereas in meditation we focus both on "divine truth" and our "own soul," contemplation means setting our mind "on the beauty and glory of God."[46] Meditation therefore has a broader scope—it encompasses our reflection on the beauty of creation, of God, Scripture, and our own sinfulness. Contemplation, however, is more specifically focusing our minds on divine things. For Edwards, contemplation was, as Strobel neatly defines it, "the pilgrim-anticipation of the beatific-glory we behold in heaven."[47] (In what follows we use the terms meditation and contemplation accordingly.)

What are we meditating on in this life? Based on our earlier observations, we delight in creation as it reflects the beautiful creator. The Niagara Falls, a beautiful sunset, a polar bear (and perhaps even Bach's Goldberg Variations or Rothko's paintings) can be "shadows" of the divine things, and they are to be valued and enjoyed as they may dimly reflect the beautiful creator God.[48] Edwards used typology to highlight the spiritual things we might find in nature.[49] William Schweitzer notes that, according to Edwards, the "entire creation was embedded with typological meaning waiting to be interpreted by those who had learned the 'language of God.'"[50] With this approach, Edwards clearly reacts against the seeds of dissonance that he thinks have been sown by Enlightenment philosophers and that were forcing God out of the world. Where the Deists saw discord, Edwards recognized harmony, Schweitzer notes: "[N]ature, Scripture, and history are all in perfect, though highly complex, harmony with themselves and with one another, and this very harmony points to the underlying reality of the beautiful divine mind."[51] Edwards himself, as he meditated on the beauty of creation, was moved to turn his thoughts to the author of the beauty he perceived. In his *Personal Narrative*, Edwards writes: "I often used to sit and view the moon, for a long time; and so in the daytime, spent

---

45. See ch. 6, "Meditation and Contemplation," in Strobel, *Formed for the Glory*, 113–42.

46. Strobel, *Formed for the Glory*, 130.

47. Strobel, *Formed for the Glory*, 133.

48. Edwards writes: "For indeed the whole outward creation, which is but the shadows of beings, is so made as to represent spiritual things." Edwards, *WJE*, 13:434.

49. See chapter 8, "Typology: Scripture, Nature, and All of Reality," in McClymond and McDermott, *Theology of Jonathan Edwards*, 116–29. For a more extensive treatment of Edwards's typology, see McDermott's recent contribution, *Everyday Glory*.

50. Schweitzer, *God is a Communicative Being*, 50.

51. Schweitzer, *God is a Communicative Being*, 145.

PART I: ENGAGING ETHICALLY WITHIN CHRISTIAN COMMUNITY

much time in viewing the clouds and sky, to behold the sweet glory of God in these things; in the meantime, singing forth with a low voice, my contemplations of the Creator and Redeemer."[52] For Edwards, meditating on the beauty of creation organically ushered into praise of the creator. Oliver Crisp and Kyle Strobel note:

> The harmony of color, shape, and sound are the echoes of an eternal harmony of love that establishes the tune of all creation. Seeing the beauty of the world does not, somehow, take our eyes off of God. Rather, by basking in the beauty of the world in relation to God, we are coming to enjoy reality as he does—as a reflection of his own infinite beauty and harmony of ideas that gives meaning to all things.[53]

Beside admiring the beauty of creation, we could, too, spend some time exploring the relationships within the Christian community as they reflect the beautiful inter-Trinitarian relationships of love and consent. Gerald McDermott observes in this respect:

> Seeing God's beauty also means that community takes on new perspective. If the source of all beauty is the Trinity, then God's beauty is relationship. In fact, God is relationship. To experience God is to participate in the inner life of the Trinity. And if God displays His beauty most vividly in His own community of Persons, then we can experience and display God's beauty only in the community of the Church, which itself is participation in the Trinitarian community because it is the Body of Christ.[54]

Here is sweet communal harmony and proportion, already now, but to be consummated fully in the time to come.[55] This dynamic eschatological motif is in fact an important element in Edwards's theology. Our experience of beauty is shaped and formed already here as we journey on earth. And as we grow up "in every way into him who is the head, into Christ" (Eph 4:15), we are being transformed, step by step, in our capacity to perceive beauty until we enter glory where we will enjoy the sublime beatific vision. While we could talk more about the beauty of creation and of harmonious relationships, I suggest we focus in more detail on the christological implications for contemplation based on our earlier observations.

52. Edwards, *WJE*, 16:794.
53. Crisp and Strobel, *Jonathan Edwards: An Introduction*, 66.
54. McDermott, "Surprised by Beauty."
55. McClymond and McDermott, *Theology of Jonathan Edwards*, 101.

This christocentric move would certainly be in Edwards's interest. For everything, in Edwards's view, is ultimately infused with the beauty of Jesus Christ. Even "when we are delighted with flowery meadows and gentle breezes of wind," Edwards writes, "we may consider that we only see the emanations of the sweet benevolence of Jesus Christ; when we behold the fragrant rose and lily, we see his love and purity."[56] Christ is the ultimate concern of our spiritual contemplation. How do we contemplate Christ? And what impact does it have on our life, experience, and perhaps even character? To these questions we turn next.

Contemplating the Beautiful Jesus Christ

We have already introduced Edwards's idea of the "new sense" that God gives the believer so that she can see the beauty of divine things. In his famous sermon of 1734, Edwards speaks of "A Divine and Supernatural Light" that is imparted to the soul by the Spirit of God that enables us to see and admire the beauty of Christ.[57] When God takes away the blindness and grants his divine and supernatural light, human eyes are wide open to a truly life-changing sight: through the work of the Holy Spirit, Christ is now the precious-One to them.[58] Suddenly, they see him for who he really is, namely the "radiance of the glory of God and the exact imprint of his nature" (Heb 1:3). "Believers truly see God the Father in the Son as they are caught up in the movement of the Spirit to bind them to the life of God."[59] Jesus Christ, then, is for Edwards the supreme object of our admiration in contemplation. The believer has found her utmost joy and satisfaction in him. "But now they have found Christ," writes Edwards, "they have found one that is excellent indeed. They see in him a real and substantial excellency."[60] Believers now join the angels in admiring the beauty of Jesus Christ:

> He is more excellent than the angels of heaven. He is amongst them for amiable and divine beauty, as the sun is among the stars. In beholding his beauty, the angels do day and night entertain

---

56. Edwards, *WJE*, 13:279.

57. See Edwards, "Divine and Supernatural Light," 105–24.

58. For Edwards's view on the regenerative work of the Holy Spirit, see Crisp and Strobel, *Jonathan Edwards: An Introduction*, 160–64.

59. Crisp and Strobel, *Jonathan Edwards: An Introduction*, 61.

60. Edwards, *WJE*, 22:289.

and feast their souls and in celebrating of it do they continually employ their praises.⁶¹

Whilst we emulate the angels in contemplating the mesmerizing beauty of Jesus Christ, we realize that our view, of course, remains imperfect on this side of the eschaton. We only see "in a mirror dimly," eagerly longing to see "face to face" (1 Cor 13:12). Still, we are called to seek God's glory in the face of Jesus Christ, and we desire, like David, to gaze upon the beauty of the Lord (Ps 27:4, 8). Yet how exactly are we supposed to do this? How are we to contemplate the beautiful Christ in everyday life? Given our hectic and noisy lives, I wonder whether some silence would help: "Be still, and know that I am God" (Ps 46:10). Edwards often sought silence and solitude "in the woods": in order to converse with God and to meditate on him and his word. Edwards reports his own episode of contemplating Christ's beauty as follows:

> Once, as I rid out into the woods for my health . . . and having lit from my horse in a retired place . . . I had a view, that for me was extraordinary, of the glory of the Son of God; as mediator between God and man; and his wonderful, great, full, pure and sweet grace and love, and meek and gentle condescension. This grace, that appeared to me so calm and sweet, appeared great above the heavens. The person of Christ appeared ineffably excellent, with an excellency great enough to swallow up all thought and conception. Which continued, as near as I can judge, about an hour; which kept me, the bigger part of the time, in a flood of tears, and weeping aloud. I felt withal, an ardency of soul to be, what I know not otherwise how to express, than to be emptied and annihilated; to lie in the dust, and to be full of Christ alone; to love him with a holy and pure love; to trust in him; to live upon him; to serve and follow him, and to be totally wrapt up in the fullness of Christ; and to be perfectly sanctified and made pure, with a divine and heavenly purity. I have several other times, had views very much of the same nature, and that have had the same effects.⁶²

Whilst not many of us today can make it a habit to "ride out into the woods," the general thrust of the idea is clear: seeking silence and solitude in the context of God's creation, where we get the chance to meditate on the beauty of God's work, the Creator himself, and our own sinfulness—always, and this is important to add, rooted in the word of God

---

61. Edwards, "There Never Was Any Love," 292.
62. Edwards, *WJE*, 16:801.

(For Edwards, meditation was always reflection on the truth revealed in Scripture. The *Personal Narrative*, in fact, includes significant reflection on individual verses of Scripture which tell about the glory of God). A closer look at Edwards's observations reveal that he speaks here on the one hand of a deep spiritual experience that ushered in a profound emotional response—"a flood of tears and weeping aloud." Quiet contemplation of God's beauty evokes religious affections.[63] On the other hand, he clearly expressed that through this contemplative experience he was assured "to be perfectly sanctified and made pure." This deserves closer inspection, for it highlights the vital link between contemplation and transformation we find in Edwards. Contemplating a beautiful work of art in a modern art gallery can surely change us, perhaps in our look at the world or our mood. To a far greater extent does beholding Christ's beauty transform us in character and temperament. This means: contemplation and transformation are two sides of the same coin. As we behold the beauty of Jesus Christ, we are being transformed into his likeness (2 Cor 3:18).

Contemplation and Transformation

Contemplation, in Edwards's view, was not simply for contemplation's sake, a form of spiritual navel-gazing. On the contrary, Edwards insisted that contemplation quite naturally leads to transformation in character. "[P]artaking in God's life of beauty, and becoming beautiful through that participation," write Crisp and Strobel, "is the grounding of Edwards's ethical thought."[64] In his sermon on the apostle Paul's phrase in 2 Cor 3:18a, "And we all, with unveiled face, beholding the glory of the Lord, are being transformed into the same image from one degree of glory to another," Edwards describes the "glory and excellency of that is seen by believers" in Christ as follows: he mentions "the excellency of his holiness," the "wonderfulness and excellency of his love," "the meekness and humility of Jesus," and the "faithfulness of Jesus Christ as Mediator and friend."[65] As God opens our eyes for the beauty of Christ, he also transforms us into the image of the beautiful Christ. Edwards therefore speaks of the "*transforming* sight of the Glory of Christ."[66] When God transforms believers gradually into the image of his

63. See Crisp and Strobel, *Jonathan Edwards: An Introduction*, 184–86.
64. Crisp and Strobel, *Jonathan Edwards: An Introduction*, 188.
65. Edwards, "72. Sermon on Second Corinthians 3:18 (1743)."
66. Edwards, "72. Sermon on Second Corinthians 3:18 (1743)," emphasis added.

beautiful Son Jesus Christ, it means that they grow more like him in character. Organically united with Christ, God will bring into fruition in them beautiful Christlike character expressions, such as "humility, meekness, love, forgiveness, and mercy."[67] This is what makes Jesus Christ beautiful, and it is what makes us beautiful, too. In Edwards's words, believers "also become holy, their hearts are purified from their filthiness . . . Christ fills them with tender love and Charity towards those that are Christ's, those that Christ died for"—Christ "makes . . . them also of a humble and lowly disposition . . . makes 'em to be of that spirit to think of others better than themselves."[68] Moreover, for Edwards, transformation entails a distinct activating element. When contemplating the beauty of Christ, debilitating lethargy gives way to industrious activity. Edwards writes:

> But when Christ arises upon them, then all things begin to revive, the will and affections begin to move, and they set about the work they have to do. They are now awakened out of their sleep: whereas they were still before, now they begin to be diligent and industrious; whereas they were silent before, now they begin to sing forth God's praises. Their graces now begin to be put into exercise, as flowers send forth a fragrancy when the sun shines upon them.[69]

This is an important point, since all too often, contemplation is disregarded by its critics due to an alleged quietist motif. Yet the passive pious quietist who sits silently in his study with the doors locked is not the contemplative believer that Edwards has in mind. Edwardsian contemplation is an exquisite foretaste of the beatific vision that results in religious affection, transformed character, and concrete action. The believer, Edwards argues, "will not only love in word and in tongue but in deed he'll show his Inward Charity by the fruits of it."[70] From Edwards's perspective, contemplation is therefore always linked to holiness. Aesthetics and ethics belong together.[71]

---

67. Edwards, *WJE*, 2:346.
68. Edwards, "72. Sermon on Second Corinthians 3:18 (1743)."
69. Edwards, *WJE*, 10:540.
70. Edwards, "72. Sermon on Second Corinthians 3:18 (1743)."
71. Edwards writes: "Whatever controversies and variety of opinions there are about the nature of virtue, yet all (excepting some skeptics who deny any real difference between virtue and vice) mean by it something *beautiful*, or rather some kind of *beauty* or excellency." *WJE*, 8:539 (emphasis original). See Crisp and Strobel, *Jonathan Edwards: An Introduction*, 188–93; Ortlund, *Edwards on the Christian Life*, 25–26.

Conclusion

Jonathan Edwards offers a creative theology of beauty that has profound implications for our spiritual experience. Creation is beautiful as it is suffused with God's glory and grace. God himself is beautiful in the intra-Trinitarian relationships of love and consent, and in the person of Jesus Christ beauty is most profoundly revealed. Jonathan Edwards encourages believers to contemplate the beautiful Christ. While a mesmerising bonfire or an impressive waterfall might captivate us, in much greater fashion are we enthralled by the beautiful Christ who is the "image of the invisible God" (Col 1:15). He is the One who is "marvellous in our eyes" (Ps 118:23; Mark 12:11). Equipped with a "new sense" of the heart through the Holy Spirit, believers rejoice in a little foretaste of the beatific vision of the beautiful Jesus Christ, whose brightness is adjusted to our fragile faculties in this life: "The manifestation of the glory of God in the person of Christ, as it were, accommodated to our apprehensions. The brightness is suited to our eyes."[72] There is much to learn from Edwards with a view to rediscovering the important spiritual practice of contemplation. Edwards also highlights the transformative effects of contemplation and thus offers a crucial corrective to quietist misunderstandings of contemplation. As we behold the beautiful Christ, we are being transformed into his likeness, in our attitudes, dispositions, and actions. For Edwards, it was always crucial whether contemplation actually resulted in a changed life. He thus did not hesitate to challenge the believers in his congregation, asking them whether the marvelous sight of "the love of Christ" has "changed your life?" "Has it made you to abhor and loath sin as the most odious thing in the world and has it made You delight in holiness?"[73] The contemplative believer welcomes these questions, gladly exploring the beauty of Christ as she is being transformed into the image of Christ from one degree of glory to another (2 Cor 3:18).

Bibliography

Balthasar, Hans Urs von. *Prayer.* Translated by A.V. Littledale. London: SPCK, 1961.
Bombaro, John J. *Jonathan Edwards's Vision of Reality: The Relationship of God in the World, Redemption, History, and the Reprobate.* Eugene, OR: Pickwick, 2012.

---

72. Edwards, *Glory and Honour of God*, 233.
73. Edwards, "72. Sermon on Second Corinthians 3:18 (1743)."

Crisp, Oliver D. "Jonathan Edwards' Panentheism." In *Jonathan Edwards as Contemporary: Essays in Honor of Sang Hyun Lee*, edited by Don Schweitzer, 107–26. New York: Peter Lang, 2010.

Crisp, Oliver D., and Kyle C. Strobel. *Jonathan Edwards: An Introduction to His Thought*. Grand Rapids: Eerdmans, 2018.

Delattre, Roland. *Beauty and Sensibility in the Thought of Jonathan Edwards: An Essay in Aesthetics and Theological Ethics*. Eugene, OR: Wipf & Stock, 2006.

Edwards, Jonathan. "A Divine and Supernatural Light Immediately Imparted to the Soul by the Spirit of God." In *A Jonathan Edwards Reader*, edited by John E. Smith et al., 105–24. New Haven: Yale University Press, 1995.

———. *The Glory and Honour of God: The Previously Unpublished Sermons of Jonathan Edwards*, edited by Michael D. McMullen, vol. 2. Nashville: Broadman & Holman, 2004.

———. "There Never Was Any Love That Could Be Paralleled with the Dying Love of Christ." In *The Blessing of God: Previously Unpublished Sermons of Jonathan Edwards*, edited by Michael D. McMullen, vol. 1, 273–95. Nashville: Broadman & Holman, 2003.

———. *The Works of Jonathan Edwards*. New Haven, CT: Yale University Press, 1957–2008. Abbreviated *WJE*, citing volume and page numbers.

———. "72. Sermon on Second Corinthians 3:18 (1743)." *Sermons, Series II, 1728–1729* (WJE Online Vol. 43).

Holmes, Stephen R. *God of Grace and God of Glory: An Account of the Theology of Jonathan Edwards*. Edinburgh: T. & T. Clark, 2000.

Lee, Sang Hyun. "Edwards and Beauty." In *Understanding Jonathan Edwards: An Introduction to America's Theologian*, edited by Gerald R. McDermott, 113–25. Oxford: Oxford University Press, 2009.

———. *The Philosophical Theology of Jonathan Edwards: The Idea of Habit and Edwards' Dynamic Vision of Reality*. Princeton, NJ: Princeton University Press, 1988.

Louie, Kin Yip. *The Beauty of the Triune God: The Theological Aesthetics of Jonathan Edwards*. Eugene, OR: Pickwick, 2013.

McClymond, Michael J., and Gerald R. McDermott. *The Theology of Jonathan Edwards*. New York: Oxford University Press, 2012.

McDermott, Gerald R. *Everyday Glory: The Revelation of God in All of Reality*. Grand Rapids: Baker Academic, 2018.

———. "Surprised by Beauty: The Theology of Jonathan Edwards." http://www.ad-ne.org/the-anglican-way/surprised-beauty-theology-jonathan-edwards/.

Mitchell, Louis J. *Jonathan Edwards on the Experience of Beauty*. Studies in Reformed Theology and History 9. Princeton, NJ: Princeton Theological Seminary, 2003.

Ortlund, Dane C. *Edwards on the Christian Life: Alive to the Beauty of God*. Wheaton, IL: Crossway, 2014.

Platinga Pauw, Amy. "The Trinity." In *The Princeton Companion to Jonathan Edwards*, edited by Sang Hyun Lee, 51–57. Princeton, NJ: Princeton University Press, 2005.

Schwanda, Tom. "'To Gaze on the Beauty of the Lord': The Evangelical Resistance and Retrieval of Contemplation." *Journal of Spiritual Formation and Soul Care* 7.1 (2014) 62–84.

Schweitzer, William M. *God is a Communicative Being: Divine Communicativeness and Harmony in the Theology of Jonathan Edwards*. London: T. & T. Clark, 2012.

Strachan, Owen, and Douglas A. Sweeney. *Jonathan Edwards on Beauty*. Chicago: Moody, 2010.

Strobel, Kyle C. "The Beauty of Christ: Edwards and Balthasar on Theological Aesthetics." In *The Ecumenical Edwards: Jonathan Edwards and the Theologians*, edited by Kyle C. Strobel, 91–109. Farnham, Surrey: Ashgate, 2015.

———. *Formed for the Glory of God: Learning from the Spiritual Practices of Jonathan Edwards*. Downers Grove: InterVarsity, 2013.

Trueman, Carl. "Why Should Thoughtful Evangelicals Read the Medieval Mystics?" *Themelios* 33, no. 1 (2008) 2–4.

4

Does Talking about Theological Ethics or Moral Theology Vaporize Christian Ethics?

Mark W. Elliott

Natural Law Giving Way to Positive Divine Law

THE SHIFT TO A "rules-based" approach to morality, whereby the canon law was stretched to legislate for lay people and clergy alike, is viewed by the majority of Catholic historians of moral theology to have been unfortunate. Now this development was untrue to the simpler teaching of Saint Thomas Aquinas: "In the teaching of Aquinas, then, the purpose of Revelation, so far as morality is concerned, appears to be essentially remedial, not absolutely necessary for man but in practice almost indispensable."[1] This would in turn then let the *natural law* of reason run life, without much recourse to revealed or positive teaching in everyday matters. Reason and the New Law on the heart through grace would lead the moral life. Yet, unfortunately, Aquinas kept Aristotle's justice as the one external cardinal virtue—controlling relationships with others—including God, in the sense of giving him his due. Jack Mahoney thinks this one step by Aquinas was a faux pas and perhaps encouraged the development of a moral theology that was altogether legal. Mahoney has strong words to say: "But to consider that this non-Christian, indeed, atheistic,

---

1. Mahoney, *Making of Moral Theology*, 107.

category of justice can be an adequate and completely enlightening means of conceptualizing and expressing the reality of man's relationship to the God of Israel and to Jesus Christ is both a travesty of the Gospel and an ignoring of the fact that all our discourse about God (and here the voluntarists have a point) is severely limited."[2] Mahoney reminds us that, in any case, we need to speak very analogically if we are going to call God a "lawgiver": he is only a lawgiver in an extremely non-literal sense.

Coupled with this voluntarism (the idea that something is good only because God willed it to be so) and loss of a sense of the inherent goodness of created nature was the emphasis on mediation of grace in all matters spiritual by the lives of saints, the eucharist, sacred art, the Protestant ministry, and sermon. One had to reach up for grace and even then God touched lives only indirectly. According to Louis Dupré, writing about the humanism of Francis de Sales, "The Salesian synthesis remains a strictly interior one, between God and the soul.... The saint obviously 'accepts the physical world'—but that does not mean that he theologically integrates it."[3] By way of contrast, Ignatius Loyola had more of a cosmic vision, taken up by the Baroque for which visual art as mediation was necessary. "Baroque culture views creation as pervaded by a natural desire of God," but this implies that God is some way off, except for the soul of a special saint or two.[4] There was also a Protestant sacralization of nature in poetry, music, and Dutch art, but bridging the invisible gap in spirituality meant admitting there was one, as creation and Creator seemed to drift apart. Eventually came "the definitive withdrawal of the transcendent dimension from Western culture," as transcendence was kicked upstairs, or as William Placher put it, domesticated.[5] With the passing of time and the influence of thinkers who put more emphasis on will than justice, that external facing of the four cardinal virtues, justice, came to be defined as "our will being conformed to the divine will."[6] God became the legislator, and Francisco Suarez spoke of the divine will as expressed in all his laws, which the church then reprinted. This necessitated that the church be infallible in faith and *mores*. The Council of Trent said this and meant by *mores* "customs." However with Suarez and other scholastics around 1600, *mores* soon became understood as morals. The church

---

2. Mahoney, *Making of Moral Theology*, 252.
3. Dupré, *Passage to Modernity*, 229.
4. Dupré, *Passage to Modernity*, 243.
5. Dupré, *Passage to Modernity*, 248; Placher, *Domestication of Transcendence*.
6. Dupré, *Passage to Modernity*, 138.

was tasked with handing down the divine will in all its details. John Bossy has famously charted how both in Protestant and Catholic circles, the seven deadly sins (as opposed to the seven or eight virtues) were abandoned in favor of the Ten Commandments to give structure to moral thinking and teaching. The dominant theme was that of will and authority rather than the struggle for personal virtue and love.

Laxism and Casuistry

Inevitably there were ways to try to soften this hard-sounding discipline, for the sake of being able to touch as many lay people as possible, even if with a very light touch. The key text was Romans 14:23: "what does not proceed from conviction is sin." πᾶν δὲ ὃ οὐκ ἐκ πίστεως ἁμαρτία ἐστίν (pan de ho ouk ek pisteōs hamartia estin). *Non ex fide omne autem quod non ex fide peccatum est.* In the Anglican tradition, Richard Hooker argued that things had changed since NT times and so such a high "apostolic" standard is educative, not obligatory: the question is (pragmatically), has the church learned from the past to rise by its own standards? We should not do what Scripture forbids, and we should do what it says; but where Scripture is silent, then reason is to be our guide (contra Cartwright's argument that whatever was not done of faith, relying on revelation alone, was sin: Rom 14:23). For Hooker this does not mean that such things that are left to reason are matters of indifference, as Melanchthon had suggested. They *are* important, for indeed reason and conscience are holy things. And here Thomas Aquinas was affirmed in his emphasis on the intention of the moral agent as per his *Quodlibet* 3 art 27: "A human act is judged to be virtuous or vicious according to which the will is imposed and not according to the material object of the act" (cf. St Bernard *De praeceptione et dispensatione* c12 and 17: to obey a prelate's instruction over against a merely written law is to act with merit.) The perplexed conscience does not sin if one is in doubt and chooses what is a lesser evil such as the transgression of a divine or human law, rather than disobey natural law. For that is to exercise faith, so it cannot be sin. Good intention is all.

To illustrate this from the horse's mouth of moral theologians, the Redemptorist Alphonsus of Liguori: "The Apostle says: 'Everything which is not of faith (namely from the dictate of conscience, as Estius and others explain), is sin (Romans 14:23).'"[7] In the case of invincible erroneous conscience where the person has no doubt, the invincibly erroneous person

---

7. Liguori, *Theologia Moralis*, 25.

acquires merit.[8] "The reason is, because to say some act is good, or at least neutral, suffices that one is directed by the dictate of reason and prudence. Therefore, since the one doing the work acts prudently, there ought to be little doubt about the good end for which it is worked, namely the glory of God or charity towards one's neighbour."[9] Actions performed with right intentions are meritorious (despite Franzoja's *Theologia Moralis* 1.1.133), and one must recall that bad thoughts are not sins.[10] Here is the rule: "those who are of a God-fearing conscience, unless they morally know for certain that they consented to a grave sin, must be judged free from sin."[11] Moreover, if a pastor counsels something, then one can licitly act. Liguori quotes St. Antoninus here: "Between a hard and favorable opinion about precepts, a favorable interpretation must be made in other proportionate matters."[12] Hence, "A probable conscience is when someone, supported by some probable opinion, forms for himself a dictate of reason from certain reflexive or concomitant principles to act licitly."[13]

This is not "probabiliorism", which means judging between moral opinions in favour of the more proveable. Mahoney dislikes probabiliorism, because it "presents a view of morality characterized by conflict and antagonism between wills."[14] "Conscience thus becomes the cockpit where one's freedom and another's law face each other as antagonists, and where it is the individual who judges whether or not his freedom must yield to law."[15] Better is *probabilism* as allowing a diversity of opinions so long as each is backed by some reputable moral theologian, and even if it is one of say ten opinions, it makes the act licit—e.g., if one steals in instalments it is not a mortal sin.

Casuistry has had a bad name for a long time. Until, that is, Albert Jonsen and Stephen Toulmin, *The Abuse of Casuistry*, who launched an apology for it against its abusers: "In closing, let us record our own votes against Pascal and in favor of the casuists and the Talmudists . . . The *abuse of casuistry*—not the misuse of case methods in moral argument, but the

---

8. Liguori, *Theologia Moralis*, 26.
9. Liguori, *Theologia Moralis*, 26.
10. Liguori, *Theologia Moralis*, 27.
11. Liguori, *Theologia Moralis*, 33–34.
12. Liguori, *Theologia Moralis*, 37.
13. Liguori, *Theologia Moralis*, 55.
14. Mahoney, *Making of Moral Theology*, 243.
15. Mahoney, *Making of Moral Theology*, 229.

insulting scorn to which they have been subject since Pascal attacked the Jesuits in *The Provincial Letters*—has been almost entirely unjustified."[16] Pascal's rhetorical tropes were modeled on maths, forgetting that ethics is about rhetorical argumentation not formal or geometrical argumentation, forgetting that we live in fallen and difficult worlds and so it is better to do the little good we can: and "yes, we can!"[17]

For, according to Jeffrey Stout, Baroque Catholic theologians with few exceptions confidently taught the ethical capability of humans.[18] Gabriel Vasquez was one such exception: he was a radical Augustinian, for all that his language sounded scholastic, with its reference to "supernatural mode" and "natural agents." There was, for Vasquez, no natural love for God; all the works of sinners are sins. However, this was resisted by most Catholic moral theologians of the time, who argued that at least for a moment all people were capable of love for God. What people could offer was at least "no obstacle" to grace (Suarez) and possibly more. Thomists/Augustinians complained against the Molinist and Suarezian distinction of sufficient/efficacious grace that either grace converted one (again and again in Aquinas's view) and was efficacious, or it did not and was therefore not sufficient. The Jesuits seemed to be putting the difference into the hands of the individual will. For the Jesuits, Molina saw the Dominicans as "Lutherizing" and Suarez sounded very "modern" in that he dealt with liberty as *real or "libertarian" freedom* (not just "freedom from sin"—Augustinian). He talked about pure nature as a state existing between grace and sin: a third position. Nature has the potential to obey—but Suarez went further—that is an *active* potential!

In Jansenist, hence, anti-Jesuit circles in France, ethics became split into the Spirit working with the weak charity of true believers, and an inferior but public morality of those without the Spirit.[19] This established "a realm of the natural in which grace is not active. Moral anatomy thus served as an instrument for human control and manipulation of self and society, rather than as training in receptivity and the discernment of grace."[20] Ironically, this was arguably the same result as that of the Jesuits, and as in the Scottish Enlightenment too, with its appreciation for a selfish yet enlightened moral sense in all humans. Again, grace gets shut out.

16. Jonsen and Toulmin, *Abuse of Casuistry*, 341.
17. Jonsen and Toulmin, *Abuse of Casuistry*, 331.
18. Stout, *Flight from Authority*.
19. Herdt, *Putting on Virtue*, 247.
20. Herdt, *Putting on Virtue*, 247.

For the spiritual life is one of not just going with the mechanical flow but of making some decisions. Freedom means not to have to submit to a fate. This freedom allows virtue to be cultivated and carry on along towards true happiness, practical and mystical, as spelled out by S. Pinckaers, for whom:

> to deny the priority given to personal moral judgement would mean no less than a denial of man's natural capacity to experience the light of objective truth and goodness through conscience or synderesis. The communication of moral truths must demand, first and foremost, an internal movement, whilst accepting the necessary, though subordinate, role of external influences of casuistic models and prescriptive morals. This approach, argues Pinckaers, promotes the growth of true freedom so that "the more moral freedom grows in this sense, thanks to the virtues, the more it is protected from the arbitrary, rejecting it so as to move toward what it loves in truth."[21]

Lessons from the Catholic Past According to Mahoney

At the end of his review of these early modern historical developments, Jack Mahoney himself gives clear signs that his preference is "more Johannine than Matthaean" in his view of NT ethics. Thus the church should look to the Spirit as internal teacher of all the faithful.[22] This analysis of the biblical material here is a bit "broad-brush," not least with its appeal to "moral communication between subjects."[23] Mahoney is impressed by Paul VI in his controversial encyclical on contraception, *Humanae Vitae*, mentioning the need for the spirit working on each heart to give assent to *Humanae Vitae*, for there is a certain authority of personal Christian experience, one which ranges widely.[24] Karl Rahner puts it: "Just because grace is *free and unmerited* this does not mean that it is rare."[25] "Actual human nature is *never* 'pure' nature, but nature in a supernatural order."[26] Yet to spin grace out this way is

21. Pinckaers, "Aquinas and Agency," 184, cited in Kane, "Servais Pinckaers," 32.
22. Mahoney, *Making of Moral Theology*, 222.
23. Mahoney, *Making of Moral Theology*, 223.
24. Mahoney, *Making of Moral Theology*, 294–95.
25. Rahner, *Nature and Grace*, 133.
26. Rahner, *Nature and Grace*, 135.

to only tell one side of the story. The other side is one which pays attention to revealed theological categories as giving shape to that spirituality out of which a more distinctly Christian ethics might spring.

As for Mahoney, his preference is for the Suarezian (or Aristotelian) idea of *epicheia*, viz., what would the legislator think of the situation he didn't foresee?[27] This assumes benign consideration. With reference to *Nicomachean Ethics* 6.10: "For Aristotle the exception, far from weakening the law actually improves and corrects it."[28] It provides a supplementary function, as new hard cases develop the law. According to Albert the Great, "one must respect the variability of the real . . . it is the rule which must be adapted to the real." The law has the quality of reason. To my ear this sounds suspiciously Hegelian, as in Hegel's *Preface to the Elements of the Philosophy of Right*: "what is rational is actual; and what is actual is rational."[29]

This puts a premium on grace, and law has to be reasonable, perhaps. But again it is onesided, without much explicit reference to God the Trinity, Jesus Christ, or the Spirit in the church among other things. In other words, not much dogma. And dogma matters because it points and leads to these important and real mysteries.

After the Second Vatican Council one could almost taste the triumph of this alternative, "new" spirituality, where spirituality and ethics (without doctrine) were sometimes fused.[30] "And to the extent that moral theology, after centuries of separation, is now drawing closer to the Church's spiritual and mystical traditions, to that extent it is experiencing a healthy corrective to its former preoccupation with law."[31] However, this seems in danger of tipping the balance into a subjectivism where too much is given to the situated decision-maker. It is one thing to quote approvingly Thomas Aquinas on the New Law, whose primary element is the presence of the Holy Spirit (*ex sicut dispositive*), and another to suggest that the Holy Spirit makes it up as he goes along and can and does revise his view on a daily or generational basis.[32]

Mahoney thinks ethical formation is about education in values rather than about occasional judgments of right and wrong. "And partly

---

27. Mahoney, *Making of Moral Theology*, 98.
28. Mahoney, *Making of Moral Theology*, 236.
29. Hegel, *Preface to the Elements of the Philosophy of Right*, 20.
30. Mahoney, *Making of Moral Theology*, 254.
31. Mahoney, *Making of Moral Theology*, 254.
32. Aquinas, *Summa Theologica*, Ia-IIæ, Q.106.

by distinguishing more clearly between moral instruction or teaching on the one hand, which is couched most frequently in categorical absolutes with distinct voluntaristic overtones, and moral education on the other hand, which seeks to probe and disclose the reality, both divine and human, which is both the source and the purpose of such teaching."[33] Yet surely it is both: formation in values (and possibly something less vague than a "divine and human reality"), the better to deliberate.[34]

Thus Mahoney is able to conclude: "It is the consideration that, as a branch of Christian theology, moral theology is concerned at heart with the mystery of God and 'the riches of the glory of this mystery' (Col 1:27), and that a renewed moral theology can find its theological identity only by a recovery of this mystery. It is the mystery of God which earths all theology and at the same time makes theological pluralism unavoidable."[35] It is interesting to think of the mystery of God as that which makes nothing any better than equally probable. There is little here about Jesus as teacher, let alone creation ethics and the commandments of biblical revelation.

Admittedly, the Jesuit tradition has a lot against which it must compete:

> The predilection for the will and the power rather than the mind of God, which is to be found by and large in Scripture, as in Augustine, Abelard, and the Franciscan tradition of Scotus and Occam, may be seen as in some sense an attempt to glorify the transcendence and majesty of God, and his supreme freedom of activity. One consequence of this is to view the divine-human relationship as a continual series of border incidents and demarcation disputes . . . Augustine . . . could conceive of divine and human action as only in competition.[36]

What Mahoney wants to get around is a spirituality that has a doctrinal backbone, that says that there are boundaries and distinctions between God and his creatures. Mahoney's is a misreading of Augustine, one whose soteriology can be encapsulated in "He who made thee without thee will not save thee without thee."[37] Augustine did speak of human cooperation with grace. And as Eric Gregory has suggested, there is a large area called the political-ethical, which Augustine is only too ready to

---

33. Mahoney, *Making of Moral Theology*, 253.
34. Mahoney, *Making of Moral Theology*, 253
35. Mahoney, *Making of Moral Theology*, 337.
36. Mahoney, *Making of Moral Theology*, 245.
37. Augustine, *Serm.* 169, 11, 13: PL 38, 923.

cede to human power under divine providence. Yet perhaps because of his positive account of human possibilities once one is a believer, a lot is made of rules, duties as well as joy: a eudaemonian *ethics*. Contra Mahoney this balance seems admirable.

Protestantism and Barth

One alternative to the Jesuit and Redemptorist casuistry, of making lots of exceptions to moral rules, was to be found in the Protestant Enlightenment. The notion of a natural law that drove (like a natural current) the rational creature towards an end of fulfillment—even in God—was replaced by an emphasis on a set of obvious and well-defined morals as originating with *society*, as Divine Providence arranged. One may even speak of a "social" anthropology, with "society" as primal: with Pufendorf. Vico, for whom history no longer had a goal, there was a retreat from purpose or teleology with its promised happy ending to history as a pathetic comfort for the soul. Instead society became the providentially provided way for freedom and moral growth: there are visible things to react to, work with, decide about. Natural law was no longer viewed as a force, nor even a tendency, but was equated to the operation of free reason. For G. Thomasius, natural law was no longer *law*. In fact it was seen to suggest duties of honour that were different from and higher than those of law, towards the formation of civil society. Only positive state law is really law usually restraining evildoers. Natural law is only advisory, and there is no institution to enforce it. John Locke agreed.[38]

Kant's insistence on a formal account of ethics, i.e., that agents looked to their rational selves rather than to any outward code before comparing notes and acting together in freedom resulted in even the great Karl Barth proposing a command theory of ethics that results in "it's between you and God" and here is a bit of wisdom on what should be enduring principles.[39] This is quite different in practice from Schleiermacher's decision to view ethics as a non-speculative discipline, built up from case histories, of how Christians have responded to situations, since his way is to tell a story of how ethics proceeds from struggle, from the competition of goods, and it

---

38. See Rohls, *Geschichte der Ethik*, 285.

39. There are fine works on Barth's Ethics including: Nimmo, *Being in Action*; Clough, *Ethics in Crisis*; Webster, *Barth's Ethics of Reconciliation*; Biggar, *The Hastening That Waits*; Migliore, ed. *Commanding Grace*.

does not arise effortlessly out of pious selfconsciousness of sin and grace, as doctrine did. Yet each story is about an encounter which when all is said and done remains subjective, as Kierkegaard said it was. Scripture as law gives us something outside of ourselves to which to respond, and yet of course it is patent of interpretation for better or for worse. Barth's preference to leave the encounter's agenda "TBA" is understandable; an ethics which takes its shape by being a mirror image of the dogmatics. Barth's 1959–60 lectures were published in 1976 and translated as *The Christian Life*—fragments at the end of the *Church Dogmatics*. There he argues that one should be careful not to identify God's will with a set of ethical principles. For that robs God of his sovereignty and personal interaction, depending on what and how God reveals. It also tends to forget the place of "reconciliation." Freedom is simply behaving as creature. Divine command relieves the fear of being for oneself and invites the human being to a personal or moral fellowship.[40] As Nigel Biggar commented in *The Hastening That Waits*: "Therefore, the command of God the Reconciler is not to be seen as suspending the orders of creation, but rather as developing them in response to new circumstances, in tandem *with humans calling on God in prayer rather than God simply calling them in vocation*."[41] What comes to the fore is the correspondence of ours to God's gracious action. Ethical reflection is like a preparation for meeting with God's command and a preparation for hearing his voice, not a replacement for that meeting.[42] But is not that to belittle ethics by subjectivizing it, even if "God" is assumed to take the initiative to which "my initiative" responds?

Stanley Hauerwas

Stanley Hauerwas too has a form of this "formalist" ethics. When it comes to content, he knows what he doesn't like. Writing about Reinhold Niebuhr in *With the Grain of the Universe*, "Justification by faith is loosed from its Christological context and made a truth to underwrite a generalized virtue of humility in order to make Christians trusted players in the liberal game of tolerance."[43] At least that old liberal William James believed in "habit." Yet it is an ethics of forgiveness and gratitude, not a moralism, and certainly

---

40. Barth, *Church Dogmatics*, vol. III/4, 261.
41. Biggar, *Hastening That Waits*, 77. My emphasis.
42. McKenny, *The Analogy of Grace*, 229.
43. Hauerwas, *With the Grain*, 136.

not a pessimism. Cowriting with Sam Wells, Hauerwas observes that for the early church, baptism meant immersion into a way of life, not into a set of ideas. "What matters is not only that the acts are of a certain kind, but that the agents have certain characteristics as they perform them."[44] When Pierre Hadot calls gospels as "training manuals for discipleship," that this is not mere moralism or even legalism is spelled out: "One of the constant temptations that has beset Christians is to believe that they are saved by Christianity rather than by the works God has accomplished in Christ."[45] Yet there is a dangerous corollary of that, namely that ethics is set outside the realm of salvation. "Hauerwas often proceeds by way of genealogical forms of argument that shake the reader's sense of certainty about their common sense notions of ethically potent but historically specific ideas such as family, childhood or old age."[46] This means he thinks Christian ethics performs a negative function of questioning our notions of the good, as being not necessarily what natural values would suggest. This then is a formal approach, light on specific, constructive content.

Rufus Black (now vice-chancellor at the University of Tasmania), in his book *Christian Moral Realism* cites Hauerwas, arguing that for this modern kind of virtue ethics, morality includes "the kind of men [sic] they are . . . the kind of beliefs they hold, and the way that they integrate and organize their resources and energies to form a coherent plan of life."[47] What is proposed is "a narrative ethic that *enables people to pursue the human wholeness and integrity* which the gospels display, by following the way of life that they depict in the face of the complexities and tragedies of human existence."[48] As Black notes, Hauerwas is not quick to mention grace. Of course a disposition to obey is good, but (according to the Catholic moral theologian Germain Grisez) sometimes one acts *despite* one's emotions, and one might be virtuous in intention, yet fail to consider all the factors, with disastrous consequences.[49] Hauerwas wants to make ethics a habit to learn or a role to master, as if having the right attitude and turning up is all that is required. Grisez's gradualism—small steps of following principles rather than Hauerwas's "character" priority—gives more than a bit of detail

---

44. Hauerwas and Wells, eds. *Christian Ethics*, 39.
45. Hauerwas and Wells, eds. *Christian Ethics*, 41.
46. Brock and Hargaden, "Afterword," 292.
47. Hauerwas, *Vision and Virtue*, 69, cited in Black, *Christian Moral Realism*, 196–97.
48. Black, *Christian Moral Realism*, 206.
49. Grisez, *The Way of the Lord*.

to the double love command of Jesus. Hauerwas's method is "unsuccessful" by tackling it from the "what shall I be?" end and the concomitant fact that this "ethics of improvisation" is "making it up as one goes along," sometimes simply needs to be corrected with "what shall I do?"[50]

Oliver O'Donovan

Oliver O'Donovan has recently revisited some of the territory mapped out in his *Resurrection and Moral Order* book from the 1980s, a book that was self-consciously metaethical or a prelude to theological ethics.[51] For the later O'Donovan too, it might not be enough for ethical deliberation simply to say, "follow Jesus." When he quotes Col 3:1 ("since then you are risen with Christ, seek the things that are above") it is quite clear that some kind of contemplation of heavenly truths is in order, *thanks to Jesus*, perhaps, but without much focus on the way of the Lord Jesus.[52] Connected to this is his statement: "Unless we know our history not merely as a narrative of origin but as a divine call, we cannot grasp our freedom."[53] The people of God are being summoned upwards. There is a mystical and vocational aspect to living ethics. If Barth believed that the Lord's Prayer was the center of the Sermon on the Mount, then for O'Donovan the "We" of the Lord's Prayer applies to all humans who stand before their heavenly father.[54]

Yet that does not free ethics as theology from needing doctrine. Au contraire, "Ethics must wait on Doctrine, content to say the second word," and in a context of praise responding to truth.[55] O'Donovan prefers to speak the language of *formation*, with the human spirit responding in sympathy to the Holy Spirit. However, this will take place in fellowship where doctrine is owned commonly whatever the various shapes and patterns of individual believing lives.[56] Having established this, it is important to take the self seriously, to consider it—not despise it with self-forgetfulness (Fénélon) yet nor fixate on it as the center of a prudent morality (self-preservation of a scholarly sort). In short, "[I]ndividual freedom shrinks

---

50. Black, *Christian Moral Realism*, 316; Hauerwas and Wells, *Christian Ethics*, 282.
51. O'Donovan, *Resurrection and Moral Order*.
52. O'Donovan, *Self, World, and Time*, 29.
53. O'Donovan, *Self, World, and Time*, 37.
54. O'Donovan, *Self, World, and Time*, 38.
55. O'Donovan, *Finding and Seeking*, 6.
56. O'Donovan, *Finding and Seeking*, 39.

if it lacks the capacity to imagine itself part of a wider common agency. It must look for the Kingdom of God."[57] This is something ever-widening that expands beyond a self-reflective clan of our own opinions. There is a radically spiritual aspect to this: We wrongly love the world when we love it as we see it; we need to love the Father so we can see the world as he sees it, including seeing things in order so as to use them properly. There is place for sorrow as the loss of the good that should preoccupy us, rather than a hatred for evil. And love does take value from its object, against Nygren and Pannenberg. For "he has shown you what is good"—including natural truth as beauty as part of revelation to all senses.[58]

In the third volume it is even more clear that there needs to be an approving community for Christian ethics to function. What is mine is ours, intentionally and personally, with Acts 20:35 as a key text. He then embarks on "ethical exegesis" of 2 Timothy 3 as well as producing a mini-commentary on Ecclesiastes. There are some fine insights: the figure of Coriolanus who was not prepared to *seek* recognition, and therein was a tragic flaw, disguised as humility: a disdain for the world ends with it being taken hostage by it.[59] In a chapter called "The Communication of Friendship," O'Donovan works with Jean-Yves Lacoste's idea that concern and coexistence is just a fact, not something *moral*; yet co-*presence* works as a promise and is moral. "We may be friendly to all (hardly moral) but we cannot be a friend to all (the moral part)."[60] However "[F]riendship with God is a moral orientation, a direction of love towards the transcendent good. Friendship with Christ, however, is a moment of fulfilment, a concrete, material encounter."[61] "The Gospel we believe is about Christ's risen presence to us, and to the extent that they focused upon this point, rejecting a Protestant tendency to reduce the Gospel to a *meaning* to be *understood*."[62] (Even if Protestants were right to ask questions about the *mode* of this presence.) "Just as Christ's dying was an act and not just an event, so too our deliberation faces the future and so faces the time of our ending," with hope.[63] The only end that we can impose is to master our stubborn unwillingness to die right now. Looking

57. O'Donovan, *Finding and Seeking*, 60.
58. O'Donovan, *Finding and Seeking*, 125.
59. O'Donovan, *Entering into Rest*, 68.
60. O'Donovan, *Entering into Rest*, 140.
61. O'Donovan, *Entering into Rest*, 153.
62. O'Donovan, *Entering into Rest*, 158.
63. O'Donovan, *Entering into Rest*, 209.

back, regrets "need to be assigned to their proper place within a coherent narrative of the sanctifying grace of God."[64] The message of resurrection allows old age to be about living, but with a hand on the intelligence of the past. The present may need those past experiences to advise it.[65] The two steps seem to be that of prayer as encounter and yet deliberation in the context of hope.

We cannot aim at the kingdom of God as we don't know its shape. We have to receive it. God sets a limit. (Happiness can be a middle-time end: so long as it is not ultimate there is a place for it.) We shuttle between the deontology of justification and the teleology of sanctification and obedience. Both the inner heart's reasons and our outer obedience matter. We move from the *De Officiis* to the *De finibus, without being* a Ciceronian! But in doing so with the faith, hope, and love of 1 Cor 13:12, or faith, love, and hope (the ancient original) as key; indeed, we move with Paul (and to some extent with Jesus). What seems clear is that love is not the first word (for "faith" is), even as it is indeed the last, in contrast with the pagan original, although it might also be the second and penultimate word, in that it is the anticipation of the kingdom as that which is ultimate. Less well known is that Paul in Romans 5 reworks the triad with peace with God as the final outcome. If Christ and the Spirit are involved in any of this, still in any case the anticipation of a hoped-for result is part of deliberation, if love is to mean anything. A Catholic position might prefer to have love as the cognitive principle with which faith then acts. Yet O'Donovan wants to be clear that faith is an answer to summons, not an echo of a naturally built-in love-participation in God. Firm and sober moral deliberation is about the narrowing down of possibility, with a goal in mind, and is in no sense "automatic." Ethics as theology, then: one might want to say "living theology" or spiritual theology—it is about witness to the Word in action less in speech although of course speech is part of living. This is why it is useful to reflect on *koinonia* as communication, not communion, in that *activity of communication*, an *agency* of a communicative, talking, relational sort is central to the enterprise. The whole of O'Donovan's account is deliberative, and conscious (of each step) without being self-conscious, and communicative, passing on tips or wisdom as one receives it. It is Augustinian in the sense of being at its best in pithy one-liners or paragraphs of oracular

---

64. O'Donovan, *Entering into Rest*, 222.
65. O'Donovan, *Entering into Rest*, 223.

wisdom rather that a relentless argument pursued through the whole work. It is that kind of spontaneous ethics, derived from ancient principles.

Liturgy and Ethics

Recently textbooks on ethics have moved to considering worship and liturgy as the foundation for the church's ethics. One thinks of Brian Brock and Bernd Wannenwetsch, not least their recent commentary on 1 Corinthians, but also of Joseph Ratzinger and in evangelical circles, by William Mattison, who writes in his epilogue: "Christians are increasingly aware of how liturgical practices are crucially formative for our practical reasoning, and so saying this book is focused on practical reasoning does not adequately justify this omission, which is acknowledged here."[66] The seven virtues are in a sense resourced by the seven petitions in the Lord's Prayers, as per Thomas Aquinas, when he gets to "Give us this day our daily bread," for prudence is the "daily bread by which we live out our lives virtuously."[67] As well as praying for literal bread, we "ask to see things more truthfully."

He might have argued instead that prudence, just as it sounds, is related to providence and is reflective of it: as we receive provision we receive prudential wisdom. There is a lot to be said for the place of liturgy in ordering desires, stilling passions, giving reorientation, confidence, and an appropriately penitent spirit. It also seems a little minimalist to rely so much on the Lord's Prayer, a central feature of most Sunday liturgies, but hardly the whole thing. There can be something terribly cerebral about much church worship, with the transcendent tamed and "kicked upstairs" like a spiritual House of Lords. God is "up there but accessible in certain ways."[68]

Rather, that mystery needs to be glimpsed in and through preaching, and readings, and singing. Also, the week ahead and "everyday life" should feature, but in such a way that the week is gathered up into the mysterious purposes of the Lord, not vice-versa, with heartfelt response of penitence for falling short of his purposes. Jesus told his disciples to baptize and make disciples, probably meaning Jews, as a penitential and messianic renewal movement. To this one might indeed add "healthy instruction and tips for sane and free Christian ethical life," but only once one has

---

66. Brock and Wannenwetsch, *Malady of the Christian Body*; Ratzinger, *Spirit of the Liturgy*; Mattison III, *Introducing Moral Theology*, 393.

67. Mattison, *Introducing Moral Theology*, 402.

68. Placher, *The Domestication of Transcendence*, 6–7.

formed the framework of worship, doctrine to lift our minds, penitence, and training in practical wisdom.

Bibliography

Barth, Karl. *Church Dogmatics*, vol. III/4, *The Doctrine of Creation*. Edited by Geoffrey William Bromiley and Thomas F. Torrance. 3rd edition. Edinburgh: T. & T. Clark, 2004.

Biggar, Nigel. *The Hastening That Waits: Karl Barth's Ethics*. Oxford: Clarendon, 1993.

Black, Rufus. *Christian Moral Realism: Natural Law, Narrative, Virtue, and the Gospel*. Oxford: Oxford University Press, 2000.

Brock, Brian, and Stanley Hauerwas. *Beginnings: Interrogating Hauerwas*. Edited by Kevin Hargaden. T. & T. Clark Enquiries in Theological Ethics. London: T. & T. Clark, 2017.

Brock, Brian, and Bernd Wannenwetsch. *The Malady of the Christian Body: A Theological Exposition of Paul's First Letter to the Corinthians*. Vol. 1. Eugene: Cascade, 2016.

Clough, David. *Ethics in Crisis: Interpreting Barth's Ethics*. Farnham: Ashgate, 2005.

Dupré, Louis. *Passage to Modernity: An Essay in the Hermeneutics of Nature and Culture*. New Haven: Yale University Press, 1993.

Grisez, Germain. *The Way of the Lord Jesus Christ*. Chicago: Franciscan, 1983.

Hauerwas, Stanley. *With the Grain of the Universe: The Church's Witness and Natural Theology*. London: SCM, 2002.

Hauerwas, Stanley, and Samuel Wells, eds. *The Blackwell Companion to Christian Ethics*. 2nd edition. Malden, MA: Blackwell, 2011.

Hegel, Georg W. F. " Preface." In *Elements of the Philosophy of Right*, edited by Allen W. Wood, 1–23. Translated by H. B. Nisbet. Cambridge: Cambridge University Press, 1991.

Herdt, Jennifer. *Putting on Virtue: The Legacy of the Splendid Vices*. Chicago: University of Chicago Press, 2008.

Jonsen, Albert R., and Stephen Toulmin. *The Abuse of Casuistry: A History of Moral Reasoning*. University of California Press, 1988.

Liguori, St. Alphonsus. *Theologia Moralis: Moral Theology Volume 1: Books I-III: On Conscience, Law, Sin and Virtue*. Translated by Ryan Grant. Post Falls: Mediatrix, 2017.

Mahoney, John. *The Making of Moral Theology: A Study of the Roman Catholic Tradition. The Martin D'Arcy Memorial Lectures 1981–1982*. Oxford: Clarendon, 1987.

Mattison, William, III. *Introducing Moral Theology: True Happiness and the Virtues*. Grand Rapids: Brazos, 2008.

McKenny, Gerald. *The Analogy of Grace: Karl Barth's Moral Theology*. Oxford: Oxford University Press, 2010.

Migliore, Daniel L., ed. *Commanding Grace: Studies in Karl Barth's Ethics*. Grand Rapids: Eerdmans, 2010.

Nimmo, Paul T. *Being in Action: The Theological Shape of Barth's Ethical Vision*. London: T. & T. Clark, 2007.

O'Donovan, Oliver. *Ethics as Theology*, vol. 1. *Self, World, and Time*. Grand Rapids: Eerdmans, 2013.

———. *Ethics as Theology*, vol. 2. *Finding and Seeking*. Grand Rapids: Eerdmans, 2014.

PART I: ENGAGING ETHICALLY WITHIN CHRISTIAN COMMUNITY

———. *Ethics as Theology*, vol. 3. *Entering into Rest*. Grand Rapids: Eerdmans, 2017.
Pinckaers, Servais. *Sources of Christian Ethics*. Translated by Sr. Mary Thomas Noble. 3rd edition. Edinburgh: T. & T. Clark, 1995.
Placher, William. *The Domestication of Transcendence*. Louisville, Westminster John Knox, 1996.
Rahner, Karl. *Nature and Grace: Dilemmas in the Modern Church*. Translated by Dinah Wharton. New York: Sheed & Ward, 1964.
Ratzinger, Joseph. *The Spirit of the Liturgy*. San Francisco: Ignatius, 2000.
Rohls, Jan. *Geschichte der Ethik*. 2., neu bearbeitete und ergänzte Auflage. Tübingen: Mohr Siebeck, 1999.
Stout, Jeffrey. *The Flight from Authority: Religion, Morality, and the Quest for Autonomy*. Notre Dame: University of Notre Dame Press, 1981.
Webster, John. *Barth's Ethics of Reconciliation*. Cambridge: Cambridge University Press, 1995.

Part II

Engaging Ethically with Wider Society

5

The Ethics of Jesus

The Paradox of Jesus's Strenuous Demands and Inclusive Lifestyle

GREG W. FORBES

Introduction: Ethics of Jesus or Ethics of the Gospels?

WHEN SPEAKING OF THE ethics of Jesus we are confronted with methodological issues at the outset. First of all, can we even talk about the ethics of Jesus when there is so much conjecture regarding the authenticity of the gospel tradition? Wouldn't it be more correct, and less contentious, to speak of the ethics of Matthew, Mark, Luke, or John? Consequently, most scholarly material on NT ethics tends to avoid any reference to the ethics of Jesus, and of those who do refer to Jesus, very few actually use him as their starting point.[1] This is, of course, the polar opposite to the popular evangelical dictum of "What would Jesus do?"

---

1. Burridge, *Imitating Jesus*, 1–32, provides a helpful summary of the literature. Hays, *Moral Vision*, begins with Paul, then works through each Gospel separately before dealing with the ethics of the historical Jesus in a brief excursus (158–68). However, Hays does appear to be a little timid, and the methodological guidelines he proposes should have allowed him to be a little more positive about the historicity of the material.

The second problem relates to the nature of the Gospels themselves. They are not (as are any of the NT books) ethical handbooks or treatises. Certainly they contain ethical issues and teaching, but in the Epistles ethics appear more as a by-product of the situation that occasioned them, whereas for the Gospels they appear as part of a larger body of teaching regarding God and his kingdom. So, to what extent is it legitimate to extract, as it were, the ethics of Jesus from this larger narrative?[2]

Both Richard Burridge and Jonathan Pennington helpfully address the above concerns with reference to the genre of the Gospels as Greco-Roman *bioi* (lives).[3] The "lives" were written to focus mainly on the public life of a notable figure, including their words and actions, culminating in their death as the climax of the subject's life and the revelation of their true character.[4] This has significant ramifications for how we understand the Gospels and their ethical content. First, "Christology is . . . the biographical key to the gospels' hermeneutic."[5] In other words, the Gospels are primarily about Jesus, not about early Christian communities. Second, the ethics of Jesus presented in the Gospels are not just distillations of the things he taught, but also a remembrance of the things that he did. In fact, it is probably more accurate to say that, in large measure, Jesus was remembered as saying certain things because he consistently acted in a manner that reinforced his teaching.[6] Again, this point is reinforced by the genre of the Gospels as *bioi*.[7] Third, although the *bioi* were not written primarily for ethical teaching, they were concerned with *mimesis* (imitation). The character of the subject, particularly at crisis points in their life, is held up as exemplary. Consequently, we would suppose that the Gospels

---

2. Burridge, *Imitating Jesus*, 16; Matera, *New Testament Ethics*, 1–10.

3. First proposed in Burridge, *What Are the Gospels?* Pennington, *Reading the Gospels Wisely*, 3–35, supports and also extends the work of Burridge. Pennington labels the Gospels as "*bioi* plus" (p. 25) and discusses how the Gospels have extended the genre in distinctive theological directions and are quite unique in offering a message of faith and salvation for the readers.

4. Burridge, *Imitating Jesus*, 24.

5. Burridge, *Imitating Jesus*, 25; also Pennington, *Reading the Gospels Wisely*, 28–29.

6. Ben Witherington III, *New Testament Theology*, 128, 167. Contrast Harvey, *Strenuous Commands*, 179, who claims that "[Jesus] was seldom remembered as having conducted himself in a way that would provide a moral example for his followers to emulate."

7. Burridge, *Imitating Jesus*, 25–28.

present Jesus in the manner they do so as to impress upon the readers the virtue of imitating their master.[8]

In addition to the genre of the Gospels as *bioi*, I offer some further considerations in support of the legitimacy of regarding the content of the Gospels as accurately reflecting the ethical teaching and deeds of Jesus, and thus the legitimacy of placing him at the center of NT ethics:

i. The teaching of Jesus and the manner in which he conducted his ministry demonstrably draw upon his Jewish heritage and mirror the concerns of the Israelite prophetic tradition. If Jesus was known as a prophet (and that is difficult to deny),[9] then the presentation of him in the Gospels is entirely consistent with this perception.

ii. The palpable lack of some key ethical concerns of the early church in the Gospels (e.g., circumcision for Gentiles, food offered to idols).[10]

iii. The fact that some key elements of the ethical teaching of Jesus are reflected in the NT Epistles written earlier than the Gospels (e.g., Romans, James) would tend to weigh against the assumption that the ethics of Jesus lie deeply buried under the agenda of the evangelists.

iv. Jesus was the instigator of the Christian faith. He started it all. There would be no Gospels or New Testament without him.[11] Therefore, if the written Gospels do not reflect the ethics of Jesus to a significant extent or, as Dale Allison has argued, if the general impression of the Jesus tradition is wrong, then we can know virtually nothing at all about the historical Jesus.[12]

Throughout this paper, I will not be engaging in any historical reconstruction of particular sayings or actions of Jesus. Apart from the general case I have made above for the essential historicity of the ethical content of the Synoptic Gospels, there are two reasons for this. My overriding concern is how the ethics of Jesus function with respect to Christian ethics today. And the truth is that when Christians seek to apply the ethics of Jesus they

---

8. Burridge, *Imitating Jesus*, 28–31; Matera, *New Testament Ethics*, 9; Pennington, *Reading the Gospels Wisely*, 33–34.

9. See, for example, Sanders, *Jesus and Judaism*; Wright, *Jesus and the Victory*, 147–97; Allison, *Millenarian Prophet*; Theissen, "Jesus As an Itinerant Teacher," 98–122; Burridge, *Imitating Jesus*, 38; Hays, *Moral Vision*, 164.

10. Witherington, *New Testament Theology*, 1:128.

11. Emphasised by Burridge, *Imitating Jesus*, 36.

12. Allison, *Millenarian Prophet*, 45–51.

read the Gospels. They do not engage in historical reconstruction in an attempt to discover any redactional overlay. The ethical teachings of Jesus that we find in the Gospels are the ethics of Jesus. No matter how simplistic this may appear to a New Testament scholar, that is reality.

Second, my particular focus is on how the ethics of Jesus, and more specifically those ethics that we would categorize as arduous or particularly arduous, operate with respect to his open association with the "sinners" and those on the fringes of society. In the material I wish to cover we find an observable coherence throughout the Synoptics, even allowing for particular redactional emphases. Although there may be scholarly conjecture about some of the finer details, there is general agreement regarding the broader picture.

So, in terms of strategy, we will begin by looking at the ethical demands of Jesus, then examine his inclusive lifestyle. We will then move on to discuss how we can integrate these features in a coherent and consistent manner, and how this might apply to using Jesus as a model for Christian ethics today.

The Arduous Demands of Jesus

Jesus's Attitude to the Law[13]

The radical demands of Jesus must first of all be viewed through the lens of his attitude to the law. The key verse is Matt 5:17–18, which only serves to pose the question, "What does Jesus actually mean by 'fulfilling the law'?" And here we encounter a dilemma. Jesus's response to the law is perplexing. At times Jesus i) keeps the law (Matt 17:24–27, payment of the temple tax; Luke 4:16, Sabbath observance); ii) intensifies the law (Matt 5:21–26, anger, not just murder; Matt 5:27–30, lust, not just adultery); iii) redefines the law (Mark 7:1–16, purity is now understood in moral not ceremonial terms); iv) abrogates the law (Matt 5:31–32, no divorce; Matt 5:33–37, do not swear oaths at all); v) endorses the law (Mark 10:17–22, rich young ruler; Luke 17:10–19, the healing of the ten lepers); vi) disregards the law (Mark 2:23–28, picking grain on the Sabbath); vii) fulfills the law in his death and resurrection (Luke 24:25–27, 44–45).

---

13. For treatments see, Matera, *New Testament Ethics*, 25–30; Martin, *Christ and the Law*; Dunn, *Jesus Remembered*, 563–83; Dunn, "Law," 501–15; *Jesus and the Law*; Loader, *Jesus' Attitude*.

THE ETHICS OF JESUS

In response to this, on the surface at least, inconsistent approach to the law, some insist that Jesus was operating with distinctions within the law such as ceremonial, civil, and moral.[14] But these are anachronistic categories; it is highly unlikely that the Jews would have operated with these distinctions, for all law was moral. Of course, it is possible that Jesus operated with some sort of distinction, but we should avoid neat categorization. To argue that he kept the moral law and disregarded the ceremonial aspects clearly ignores the command he gave to the ten lepers to show themselves to the priests (Luke 17:11–19).

More relevant is the distinction between the written torah and the oral tradition (*halakah*). With respect to the latter, it weighed people down with intolerable burdens (Matt 23:4) and often neglected the weightier matters of the law (Mark 7:9–13). Yet it is not at all clear that Jesus totally disregarded all aspects of the oral law, and on the other hand there were some aspects of the written torah that he abrogated (see above).

With respect to the matters at hand, it is evident that Jesus operated as one who had authority over the law, and his varied responses to the law were in some sense a function of this authority. Undeniably, some of these responses fall under the category of "strenuous."[15] His intensification of the law to include thoughts not just actions, his redefinition of purity as moral rather than ceremonial, and the absolutism of the commands against divorce[16] and swearing of oaths were stringent requirements that many have deemed to be bordering on the impossible.

Other Radical Demands

Outside of matters explicitly related to the law we find other rigorous ethical injunctions, often in the Sermon on the Mount: rejoice when you are insulted or persecuted (Matt 5:11–12); give to anyone who asks from you, and if someone wants to sue you, give them something extra (Matt

---

14. For example, Matera, *New Testament Ethics*, 26, believes that Mark's Gospel "belongs to a tradition that distinguishes between the moral and cultic aspects of the law." However, there does not appear to be enough evidence in Mark to make such a wide-ranging assertion.

15. A term taken from Harvey, *Strenuous Commands*.

16. Most, correctly in my opinion, regard the Matthean exemption clause as secondary. For a discussion, see Hagner, *Matthew 1–13*, 122–26.

5:40–42); do not worry about having enough food, drink, or clothing (Matt 6:25–34); and do not judge anyone (Matt 7:1).

Moving beyond the Sermon on the Mount we are continually confronted with rigorous ethics. There are plenty of tough statements regarding wealth and possessions (Matt 6:24; Luke 12:33; 14:33; 16:13), and although many of the tougher ones come from Luke's Gospel, there is little doubt that teaching of this nature originated with the historical Jesus. Jesus called people to renounce everything in order to follow him (Mark 8:34–35) and expressed an urgency in this respect that even takes precedence over burying the dead or farewelling one's family (Luke 9:59–62). People should not invite their family, friends, or rich neighbours to meals, but rather the lame, crippled, and blind (Luke 14:12–14). The cost of following Jesus takes higher priority than family (Mark 3:31–35), and in the Lukan version of a Q saying this is expressed in terms of "hating one's family, and even one's own life" (Luke 14:25–27; cf. Matt 10:37). Forgiveness of others must be unlimited (Matt 18:21–22; Luke 17:3–4),[17] otherwise one cannot expect God's forgiveness for oneself.

There are also strong statements regarding judgment (Matt 7:1; 13:36–43, 47–50; 25:41–46; Mark 8:35–38; Luke 12:35–59; 13:1–9),[18] and although we find more on the need for repentance in Luke's Gospel (Luke 5:32; 13:1–5; 24:47), there seems little doubt that Jesus called people to repentance, and this call was expressed with a sense of urgency given the arrival of the kingdom.[19] It is a key feature of the Markan programmatic statement in 1:14–15 (cf. Matt 4:17) and reinforced in the mission of the Twelve (Mark 6:12).

Interpretive Issues

Obviously there are interpretive issues bound up with some of these sayings. Hating one's family is a classic case of Semitic hyperbole, where "hating"

---

17. This is the sense whether we adopt the Lukan "seven times a day," or the Matthean "seventy times seven."

18. Some of the statements occur in parable framework (interpretation) and are regarded by many as secondary. However, this is a legacy of Jülicher's allergic reaction to allegory, and an outright rejection of allegorical interpretation flies in the face of the use of allegory not only in Jewish parables (OT and Rabbis) but also in the wider Greco-Roman world (see Forbes, "Parables," 354–72).

19. Matera, *New Testament Ethics*, 20–22.

signifies to love less.[20] Hyperbole also accounts for the command to pluck out one's eye or cut off one's hand if it causes you to stumble, and for the camel through the eye of a needle analogy regarding the rich entering the kingdom of God. But there are less clear cases. What about the command to give to everyone who asks you, or the statement that calling someone a "fool" brings the danger of hellfire? Are these hyperbolic statements or simply radical demands?[21] Or may they be designed to "raise the level of moral consciousness"[22] rather than inculcate authoritative practices?

There is also the question of idealism; seemingly impossible standards evident in the statements regarding never entertaining a lustful look or angry thought, and nowhere more apparent than in the final statement of the Antitheses—"be perfect, therefore, as your heavenly Father is perfect" (Matt 5:48). It is a dangerous practice to legislate for anything other than perfection, but from a human point of view, seemingly impossible standards can create a sense of frustration and guilt.[23]

With respect to the idealism of Jesus's ethical teaching, two points can be made at the outset. First, as one who taught in the vein of the wisdom teachers and philosophical moralists of his age, we should expect generalization, exaggeration, and even confrontation rather than legal precepts and tight definition.[24] Second, his ethics must be understood with respect to the kingdom of God and the associated issue of to whom the teaching is addressed. Taking the Sermon on the Mount in an illustrative sense, the

20. Bock, *Luke 9:51—24:53*, 1284–86.

21. Burridge, *Imitating Jesus*, 52, warns "an appeal to Jesus' exaggerated style speaking as a way of avoiding the challenge of his rigorous ethic seems too easy an answer."

22. Harvey, *Strenuous Commands*, 62.

23. Throughout the history of the church the seemingly impossible standards have been dealt with in various ways. Some have advocated a two-tier discipleship, with the difficult commands embraced by those who sought perfection, whereas the masses lived by the more ordinary commands (this tendency is evident as early as the *Didache* [6.2]). In many cases this has led to a sectarian withdrawal from society. Luther made the distinction between one's private life and responsibilities to wider society (the two kingdoms approach). Others have taken a historical approach (the commands are only relevant for a certain time period—Schweitzer), or a sociological approach (they are relevant for a particular group such as itinerant missionaries). See Harvey, *Strenuous Commands*, 1–21; Burridge, *Imitating Jesus*, 58–61, for an overview.

24. Harvey, *Strenuous Commands*, 37–67. See also Pennington, *Sermon on the Mount*, 29–40. Although Pennington focuses more on Matthew's crafting of the sermon rather than Jesus as a teacher per se, his discussion of the Greco-Roman virtue tradition as a background for the material in the sermon is helpful in highlighting connections with the perspectives and interests of Greek moral philosophy.

matter of audience is complicated by the fact that the crowds are addressed in 5:1, and appear again in 7:28–29, but the disciples appear to be the focus of the teaching in at least the initial part of the Sermon. In terms of the relationship between Jesus's ethical teaching and the kingdom of God it will suffice here to state four things: i) his ethics must be understood in terms of what was to happen regarding the fulfillment of his mission at the cross.[25] The cross provides the entry point to the kingdom, whereas the ethics of Jesus demonstrate kingdom life; ii) following on from the first point, the ethical teaching that Jesus propounds is not to be understood as the criteria for becoming a disciple, or of entry to the kingdom of God; iii) the crowds overhear, and in their overhearing they are therefore made cognizant of what being a kingdom disciple entails; [26] and iv) Jesus's ethics are not designed to create a utopian society, in fact they are not meant for society at large[27] (this has important implications for the relationship between church and society in our own context).

With respect to the relationship between eschatology and the ethics of Jesus, Albert Schweitzer was both right and wrong. He was wrong in the sense that Jesus's ethics were not an "interim ethic" designed for a short span of time before the end of all things. But he was correct in insisting that Jesus's teaching was governed by the reality of the future kingdom.[28] In other words, the kingdom as both present yet future is the key to understanding the ethics of Jesus, particularly the seemingly impossible standard set by the Sermon on the Mount. The idealism relates to life perfected in the coming kingdom, and as disciples of the kingdom the followers of Jesus must strive to attain the ideal even though they will fall short of it.

Interpretive issues aside, there is little contention that Jesus's demands were rigorous and uncompromising. If so, how do we see this rigor reflected in his interactions with the people around him, particularly when he moves outside of the circle of his followers and into the larger Jewish populace?

Jesus's Inclusive Lifestyle

It is one of the axioms of historical Jesus studies that Jesus habitually associated with "sinners" and those on the margins of Jewish society. It was this

25. Witherington, *New Testament Theology*, 1:63–170.
26. Witherington, *New Testament Theology*, 1:133–34.
27. Matera, *New Testament Ethics*, 9–10.
28. Matera, *New Testament Ethics*, 18–30.

THE ETHICS OF JESUS

"open commensality," as John Dominic Crossan labels it,[29] that angered the religious establishment and was arguably one of the reasons for his eventual arrest.[30] In the Gospels we find Jesus's association with the marginalized mentioned regularly, both in summary statements about his dining habits (Matt 11:19 // Luke 7:34; Luke 15:1–3), and specific instances where he associates with such people (Matt 9:10 // Mark 2:15–16 // Luke 5:29; Luke 19:1–10; cf. Mark 7:24–30; John 4:1–26) or welcomes them (Luke 7:36–50). All this was entirely in accord with his own teaching (Luke 14:12–14).

Jesus not only associated with the marginalized, he told parables about the marginalized who are welcomed and accepted by God (Rich Man and Lazarus, Great Feast, Pharisee and Tax Collector). In fact, he considered that the welcoming of the outcasts of society was a fundamental part of his mission (Matt 9:13; Mark 2:17; Luke 4:18–19; 5:32).

Jesus's inclusive lifestyle was not confined to table fellowship but involved a willingness to heal all who came to him (Matt 8:16), whether that affliction was physical or demonic. For those considered unclean, it was not a case of Jesus risking ritual defilement, but rather of him transmitting his contagious purity.[31] Burridge states, "thus Jesus' healing ministry can be seen as an activity consistent with his general acceptance of ordinary people and even sinners and his habit of eating with them."[32]

But here we encounter an enigma. As Burridge has noted, if any Jewish group was going to feel uncomfortable around Jesus, given the rigor of his ethical teaching, it was those who had loose sexual ethics (prostitutes), or those who gained wealth from unethical financial dealings (tax collectors). Yet it is these groups who appear most at ease around Jesus, and those most threatened are the religious establishment—those who were most concerned to guard moral standards![33]

There is a further paradox when we observe what Jesus actually says to such people when he associates with them. For although, as we have seen above, Jesus's teaching regarding discipleship was extremely demanding, we find no such demands given in the context of his free association with tax collectors and sinners. They are welcomed; they are neither rebuked or subjected to any strenuous demands. In fact, the only teaching we find from

29. Crossan, *Historical Jesus*, 261–64.
30. Burridge, *Imitating Jesus*, 63.
31. See Blomberg, *Contagious Holiness*.
32. Burridge, *Imitating Jesus*, 66.
33. Burridge, *Imitating Jesus*, 62–65.

Jesus in the context of his association with them is a rebuke of those who are critical of him for so doing. The fickleness of his contemporary generation in not recognizing the wisdom of Jesus's association with tax collectors and "sinners" is chided via the simile of children in the marketplace (Matt 11:16–19 // Luke 7:31–35). The teachers of the law are admonished through the metaphor of the sick needing a doctor, not the well (Mark 2:16–17), and a similar group receive a series of three parables in Luke 15 designed not only to defend the actions of Jesus in seeking the lost (tax collectors and sinners), but also to correct their distorted view of God.[34] Simon the Pharisee is rebuked both directly and through parable for his judgmental attitude to Jesus accepting the anointing of the sinful woman (Luke 7:36–50). In going to Zacchaeus's house, Jesus says nothing to him regarding his dubious ethics, but instead pronounces salvation when Zacchaeus decides to give away half of his possessions. This is particularly interesting given the earlier command to give away "everything" (14:33), a necessity repeated in the preceding story of the rich ruler (18:18–30).

We find a similar scenario in the parable of the Pharisee and the Tax Collector (Luke 18:9–14). Here the tax collector is justified in the sight of God without offering any form of restitution but simply on the basis of a plea for propitiation (Luke 18:9–14). This was contrary to Jewish views of repentance which demanded restitution as the basis for forgiveness and acceptance.[35] While we must recognize that parables are not theological treatises and do not give the total picture of how one enters the kingdom of God, what is clear here is that God does not demand any particular actions that qualify one to repent.

Paradox or ?

So, how are we to understand the apparent contradiction between Jesus's rigorous ethical teaching on the one hand, and his free, non-demanding association with the ethically compromised of society on the other? This is not just a question that relates to the study of the historical Jesus, or an academic pursuit of the Gospels. Rather, it has a direct impact on the response of Christians to contemporary ethical questions and situations. But we will return to the present-day implications shortly.

---

34. See Forbes, *God of Old*, 109–151.

35. See Forbes, *God of Old*, 211–21. The normal translation of "mercy" by most English versions is too weak.

THE ETHICS OF JESUS

The first thing we can say is that the ethical demands of Jesus are not a condition to begin the journey of discipleship. Peter, Andrew, James, and John are simply called to follow, and are given no strenuous demands as a prerequisite (Mark 1:16–20). Even more noteworthy is the unconditional calling of Levi, a tax collector for whom Jesus's teaching regarding financial ethics would be most apt (Mark 2:13–14). The appointing of the twelve apostles is similarly not based on any stringent ethical requirement but their task is defined as "to be with him, and to be sent out to proclaim the message and to have authority to cast out demons" (Mark 3:13–15). The one obvious exception to this would be the rich man who is commanded to sell his possessions prior to following Jesus (Mark 10:17–22). But this command occurs in response to the question posed by the man regarding what he must do to attain eternal life. In this case his possessions needed to be relinquished as they were a barrier to the preeminent requirement to follow Jesus.

In light of the above, Jesus's free association with the disreputable of society is more readily appreciated. His table fellowship with them functioned as an open invitation to begin the process of discipleship, and was a parabolic statement to the effect that contrary to the contempt they received from many of their fellow Jews, they were loved and welcomed by God. In this sense, the priorities Jesus exhibited were contrary to the religious establishment, thereby explaining their incredulity and opposition. They would not have denied anyone the right to repent, but insisted that repentance needed to be demonstrated tangibly and as a prerequisite to acceptance (by them and God).[36]

Once the journey of discipleship has begun, however, the cost is clear and demanding. Metaphorically stated as "taking up one's cross" (Mark 8:34), the requirement is one of fully-fledged commitment to the kingdom and its priorities, a commitment involving an often radical adjustment in ethical behavior and moral outlook. There is no sense though that Jesus demanded such a transformation instantly (the Twelve themselves would have been in serious trouble), but perfection is the ideal to which all should aspire. We have already noted how Jesus, as a charismatic wisdom and moral teacher, is less concerned to lay down legal precepts than to offer a transformative vision, and it is with this in mind that the yoke of discipleship was to be embraced without fear of inadequacy or failure.

---

36. See the discussion in Forbes, *God of Old*, 290–95.

So, what appears to be paradoxical on the surface is readily understood by means of the nature of Jesus's mission and his priorities regarding discipleship. All can enter the kingdom, including those ostracized and even ridiculed by society. The invitation is free; there is no prerequisite. Nevertheless, once the invitation is accepted, the journey of discipleship, with its uncompromising demands, is set in motion with the ultimate goal of perfection.

The Implication for Christian Ethics Today[37]

Perhaps it is best here to proceed by way of example. Australia recently held a plebiscite regarding same-sex marriage. Not only was society deeply divided on the issue, but Christians were also vocal in their support for both positions. How can those who are supposedly working from a common ethical framework reach such vastly different conclusions on the matter? To be sure, there are a number of issues in play here, including the desire to uphold traditional values, the need to be culturally relevant and/or culturally accepted, and the nature of the church-state relationship. Nevertheless, it is also apparent that Christians on both sides of the debate invoke Jesus as support. Despite the odd eisegetical fantasy that has Jesus supporting same-sex marriage,[38] Christians generally do not look at specific statements that Jesus made that might impinge on this issue, but take a more holistic look at his life and ministry. On the one hand, those who support same-sex marriage point to Jesus's inclusive lifestyle and open acceptance of the marginalized. On the other hand, those in favor of traditional marriage point to the rigorous sexual ethics of Jesus including his statement about male and female pairing in marriage (Matt 19:5).

We have already seen that these two elements of the teaching and ministry of Jesus must be held in tension, and require a particularly nuanced appreciation. To invoke one of these elements in support of a certain position does not do justice to the complexity of the issue and is an exercise in reductionism. Yes, it is the case that Jesus associated freely with the marginalized and welcomed them unconditionally, but that is not the same as saying that discipleship was unconditional. On the other hand, Jesus's ethics are given to those who would embrace the kingdom and follow him, and

---

37. I am indebted to Burridge, *Imitating Jesus*, 78–79, for the idea. Burridge acknowledges the problem but does not develop it concretely by way of example.

38. See Cowdell, "Why 'Traditional Marriage.'"

therefore cannot be imposed on those who do not. And so, by extension, we may say that inclusivity should operate with respect to those outside the church, and stringent discipleship should operate with respect to those inside the church. Unfortunately, the reverse is often the case. Notice here that I am not arguing that Christians should have taken a particular stand on the same-sex marriage issue in the plebiscite. In being asked for our opinion by a secular government we have the right to voice it, bearing in mind the complexity of the issues involved. My main point here is with questionable and inappropriate utilizing of Jesus in the debate.

We can briefly develop this same point with respect to interfaith dialogue. On the one hand, Christians who support a more universalist position work from the basis of the inclusivity of Jesus. On the other hand, those who stress the uniqueness of Jesus and the single path of salvation work from the basis of his self-claims and radical demands. Again, we need to beware of reductionism. The free association of Jesus was meant to draw people into the kingdom, of which he was God's appointed agent to bring to fulfillment. Christians who appeal to Jesus in segregating themselves from other faiths are just as misguided as those who appeal to Jesus in openly endorsing and encouraging the meaningfulness and legitimacy of other religious systems.

In conclusion, the tension between law and grace is one that most people find difficult to navigate. With respect to the ministry and teaching of Jesus this tension is evident in his free association with the marginalized and his uncompromising, strenuous ethical demands. If Jesus is to be invoked as the basis for Christian ethics today, then a careful consideration of contextual factors, together with an appreciation of how both these strands function under the umbrella of the kingdom of God, are crucial to avoid reductionism.

Bibliography

Allison, Dale C. *Jesus of Nazareth: Millenarian Prophet*. Minneapolis: Fortress, 1998.
Banks, Robert. *Jesus and the Law in the Synoptic Tradition*. SNTSMS 28. Cambridge: Cambridge University Press, 1975.
Blomberg, Craig L. *Contagious Holiness: Jesus' Meals with Sinners*. Downers Grove: IVP, 2005.
Bock, Darrell. *Luke 9:51–24:53*. BECNT. Grand Rapids: Baker, 1996.
Burridge, Richard A. *Imitating Jesus: An Inclusive Approach to New Testament Ethics*. Grand Rapids: Eerdmans, 2007.

———. *What Are the Gospels? A Comparison with Graeco-Roman Biography*. SNTSMS 70. Cambridge: Cambridge University Press, 1992.

Cowdell, Scott. "Why 'Traditional Marriage' Has Room for Same-Sex Couples: A Theological Perspective." *ABC Religion and Ethics* (August 24, 2017). http://www.abc.net.au/religion/articles/2017/08/24/4723712.htm.

Crossan, John Dominic. *The Historical Jesus: The Life of a Mediterranean Jewish Peasant*. San Francisco: Harper & Collins, 1991.

Dunn, James D. G. *Jesus Remembered: Christianity in the Making*. Vol. 1. Grand Rapids: Eerdmans, 2003.

———. "Law." In *Dictionary of Jesus and the Gospels*, edited by Joel B. Green et al., 501–15. Downers Grove: IVP Academic, 2013.

Forbes, Greg W. *The God of Old: The Role of the Lukan Parables in the Purpose of Luke's Gospel*. JSNTSup 198. Sheffield: Sheffield Academic, 2000.

———. "The Parables." In *The Content and Setting of the Gospel Tradition*, edited by Mark Harding and Alanna Nobbs. Grand Rapids: Eerdmans, 2010.

Hagner, Donald A. *Matthew 1–13*. WBC 33A. Dallas: Word, 1993.

Harvey, A. E. *Strenuous Commands: The Ethic of Jesus*. London: SCM, 1990.

Hays, Richard B. *The Moral Vision of the New Testament: A Contemporary Introduction to New Testament Ethics*. New York: HarperOne, 1996.

Loader, William. *Jesus' Attitude Towards the Law: A Study of the Gospels*. WUNT 2/97. Tübingen: Mohr Siebeck, 1997.

Martin, Brice L. *Christ and the Law in Matthew*. Eugene, OR: Wipf & Stock, 2001.

Matera, Frank J. *New Testament Ethics: The Legacies of Jesus and Paul*. Louisville: Westminster John Knox, 1996.

Pennington, Jonathan T. *Reading the Gospels Wisely: A Narrative and Theological Introduction*. Grand Rapids: Baker Academic, 2012.

———. *The Sermon on the Mount and Human Flourishing: A Theological Commentary*. Grand Rapids: Baker Academic, 2017.

Sanders, E. P. *Jesus and Judaism*. London: SCM, 1985.

Theissen, Gerd. "Jesus As an Itinerant Teacher." In *Jesus Research: An International Perspective*, edited by James H. Charlesworth and Petr Pokorny, 98–122. Grand Rapids: Eerdmans, 2009.

Witherington, Ben, III. *New Testament Theology and Ethics*. Vol. 1. Downers Grove: IVP Academic, 2016.

Wright, N. T. *Jesus and the Victory of God*. London: SPCK, 1996.

6

Islam and Homosexuality

The People of Lot in Text and Community

BERNIE POWER AND PETER RIDDELL[1]

Introduction

WHEN THE US SUPREME Court ruled in favor of same-sex marriage in 2015, Saudi Arabia swiftly signalled its displeasure. A school in the Saudi capital, Riyadh, with a preexisting rainbow symbol painted on its building was fined US$26,000 and one of its administrators jailed. Their crime? Displaying "the emblem of the homosexuals."[2] In nearby Syria, ISIS became infamous for throwing those accused of homosexuality off tall buildings to their deaths.[3] They claimed that this followed the example of their prophet Muhammad. However, in many Muslim countries, homosexual activity is widespread. It is joked that birds fly over Kandahar in Afghanistan with one wing held under their tail as a precaution against the supposed prevalence of homosexuality.[4] It is an open secret that, besides a now repainted school, Riyadh also has several underground gay clubs. Istanbul is today one of the great cities of the Muslim world. It is located at the junction of Europe

1. Note from the editors: This article contains sexually explicit themes.
2. Whitaker, "Everything You Need."
3. Cowburn, "Isis Has Killed."
4. Whitaker, "Everything You Need."

and Asia, providing an important entry point to Turkey's 99 percent majority Muslim population and to the rest of the largely Muslim Middle East. Istanbul plays host to the largest gay pride celebration in the Muslim world. In 2003, the first gay pride March was held in Istanbul, attracting barely thirty people. By contrast, the gay pride parade in Istanbul on 30 June 2017 attracted around one hundred thousand participants and onlookers, reflecting increasing support for the event over the years.[5] This seemingly relentless growth has not been without its problems, however. The increasingly Islamist governing regime under Turkish President Recep Tayyip Erdoğan has sought to disrupt the annual gay pride parade in Istanbul, with the event being banned by local authorities since 2015. Those hardy participants who have chosen to ignore the ban have been subjected by the police to water cannon and rubber bullets each year.

A tension clearly exists in diverse Muslim communities between more liberal attitudes towards gay rights among some Muslims and more conservative attitudes among others. At a time when liberal democracies in the West are increasingly open to affirming homosexual lifestyles—consider same-sex marriage legalization in Ireland (2015) and Australia (2017)—it seems that authorities in Saudi Arabia and Turkey are leading the way in opposing liberal attitudes among Turks and the Saudis, respectively. In the following pages we will first consider the textual foundations of conservative attitudes towards homosexuality. We will then proceed to explore the incidence of homosexual activity throughout the history of Islamic communities. This will provide ingredients for gaining a greater understanding of the situation today.

The People of Lot

What of Islam's most sacred text, the Qur'an, considered by Muslims to contain the very word of God, without error or human alteration? We will turn our attention to what the Qur'an has to say about homosexuality, with particular reference to attitudes and practice of homosexuality among males, and we will fill out the discussion by reference to the vast literature that surrounds the Qur'an, in the form of commentaries, both classical and modern. A common description of homosexuals in the Arab world today is "the people of Lot." So who are the people of Lot? The answer is found in a narrative which traces its origins to the book of Genesis, where the account

5. "Istanbul Pride."

of Abraham's migration to Canaan, and his nephew Lot's encounter with the cities of Sodom and Gomorrah, is described in great detail. The Islamic version of this account is widely distributed throughout its literature.

The Qur'an on Lot and His People

References to Lot appear in a wide variety of verses and chapters, as follows: 6:86; 7:80; 11:70–89; 15:59–68; 21:71, 74; 22:43; 26:160–67; 27:54, 56; 29:26–33; 37:133; 38:13; 50:13; 54:33, 34; 66:10. For our discussion we will focus upon two sets of Qur'an verses: Q7:80–84 and Q26:165–66. These verses are a good representation of the broader set of Qur'an references listed above, and employ many pejorative words to refer to homosexual behavior.

Q7:80–84

We draw on the English translation by al-Hilali and Khan, the official English rendering produced by Islamic authorities in Saudi Arabia, which translates these verses as follows:

> 80. And (remember) Lut (Lot), when he said to his people: "Do you commit the worst sin such as none preceding you has committed in the *'Alamin* (mankind and jinns)? 81. "Verily, you practise your lusts on men instead of women. Nay, but you are a people transgressing beyond bounds (by committing great sins)." 82. And the answer of his people was only that they said: "Drive them out of your town, these are indeed men who want to be pure (from sins)!" 83. Then We saved him and his family, except his wife; she was of those who remained behind (in the torment). 84. And We rained down on them a rain (of stones). Then see what was the end of the *Mujrimun* (criminals, polytheists, sinners, etc.).[6]

Although the phrase translated as "practise your lust on men" simply means "approach men" in Arabic, this is a clear reference to sexual acts (cf. Q2:223 "approach your tilth," i.e. wives). The message is consistent. The story of Lot is a story of sin and transgression without precedent, with those guilty of these sins described as "criminals." In seeking to gain a full understanding of the meaning of Qur'an verses, it is necessary to engage with the exegetical tradition, a vast corpus of material dating back to the

---

6. Al-Hilali and Khan, *Meanings of The Noble Qur'an*.

early centuries of Islam. For this purpose, we will focus especially on a few commentaries that come from different periods and different geographical locations. The prominent classical commentary known as the Jalalayn, composed by Jalal al-Din al-Mahalli (d. 1459) and Jalal al-Din al-Suyuti (d. 1505), does not mince its words in explaining these verses:[7]

> (And) mention (Lot... when he said to his people "Do you commit abomination) that is penetrating the rears of men (such as no one in all the worlds ever committed before you humans or jinn?" ... come lustfully to men instead of women? Nay you are a wanton folk *transgressing*) ... the bounds going from what is lawful to what is unlawful. (So We delivered him and his family except his wife; she was of those who stayed behind) who remained in the chastisement. (And We rained upon them a rain) the stones of baked clay *hijārat al-sijjīl* and it destroyed them. (So behold what was the end of the *sinners*!)[8]

The Jalalayn commentary is a product of the classical Islamic world, appearing in medieval times. It is arguably the most widely dispersed commentary on the Qur'an in terms of history and geographical distribution. But does its message still ring true in the modern age?

To answer that question we will turn to the widely used twentieth-century exegete from India/Pakistan, Abul A'la Maududi (d. 1979). His lengthy commentary on the whole Qur'an often provides a perspective that relates to modern contexts, as can clearly be seen in his commentary on Q7:80–84:

> At other places, the Qur'an mentions some other crimes of these people, but here it mentions only their *most heinous crime* that brought about the scourge of Allah on them. ... Although wicked people have always been committing this most heinous sin that has given the people of Sodom an everlasting notoriety, yet it has always been considered *a filthy and detestable act*. But the only people who have ever tried to raise it to a moral excellence, were the Greek philosophers in the ancient world, and the Europeans in the modern world. The latter are doing their utmost to make up the deficiency by making an open propaganda for it, and have succeeded in giving this filthy act a legal sanction. So much so that the legislatures of some countries have legalized it. It does not require

---

7. We have included translation of Qur'anic text within parentheses for ease of reference.

8. Al-Mahalli and al-Suyuti, *Tafsir al-Jalalayn* (emphasis added).

elaborate argument to show that homosexuality is *a horrible social crime* and a heinous sin. For the Creator has made the male and the female of each and every living species different . . . to serve another purpose. This is to urge the two to live together in order to form a family along with their offspring. For this is the foundation of a civilized life for which man has been created. That is why their bodies have been made complementary to attract each other for the satisfaction of sex urges and for the service of the natural function of reproduction of the species.[9]

The above two quotations are taken from Qur'an commentaries that are five centuries apart in time and from two very different cultural contexts. Nevertheless, there are some striking resemblances. In terms of pejorative language, both are scathing in their condemnation of homosexual practice. For the Jalalayn, it is an "abomination" that earned its practitioners appropriate punishment. For Maududi, writing in the late twentieth century, homosexual practice is a "most heinous crime and sin"; it is a "filthy and detestable act" which goes against the very creative act by God which kept men and women separate and different. However, Maududi goes beyond the pejorative language of the Jalalayn to ground his discussion very much in the second half of the twentieth century, which witnessed the rise of the language of individual liberty and human rights, especially in the West, an offshoot of which was the emergence of the gay rights movement. Maududi is clearly standing against this movement in this particular portion of commentary. This snapshot of polarization between gay rights and conservative Muslim backlash is a window into the very opposition discussed at the outset of this paper in modern Turkey.

Before proceeding on with discussion of the next set of verses, it is appropriate to consider the commentary by the highly influential twentieth-century Egyptian Islamic scholar, Sayyid Qutb. Maududi and Qutb served as the two poles of twentieth-century radical Islamist thinking. They can be considered as pioneering voices in the worldwide Islamic resurgence which has been underway since the 1970s. Commenting on Q7:80–84, Sayyid Qutb has the following to say:

> Perversion of human nature is presented so clearly in the story of Lot's people. It is clear that Lot, the Prophet, does not mince words about the fact that they are the abnormal ones among God's creation, and that their *ugly perversion* is unprecedented. . . . The

---

9. Maududi, "Tafhim al-Qur'an" (emphasis added).

nature of the faith on which a particular system is based has a decisive influence in this respect. We need only to look at contemporary jahiliyyah in Europe and America to find the same sexual perversion rapidly increasing. No justification may be advanced for it other than the fact that people there have *deviated* from the right beliefs and the way of life that can be based on them.[10]

Qutb and Maududi were contemporaries and ideological soul mates, yet they were writing in very different social contexts and were addressing somewhat different primary audiences, the former Arab and the latter Indian/Pakistani. The messages strike a similar tone of lamenting the spread of "abnormal" behavior, and pointing the finger squarely at the West, chiefly "Europe and America."

Q26:165–69

These verses belong within a set of sixteen verses that repeat the pericope about Lot and his people described above. Lot challenges the people of Sodom to change their homosexual practice, warning them of dire consequences:

> 165. "Go you in unto the males of the *'Alamin* (mankind), 166. "And leave those whom Allah has created for you to be your wives? Nay, you are a trespassing people!" 167. They said: "If you cease not, O Lout (Lot)! Verily, you will be one of those who are driven out!" 168. He said: "I am, indeed, of those who disapprove with severe anger and fury your (this evil) action (of sodomy). 169. "My Lord! Save me and my family from what they do."

Turning again to the commentators, we find the same expanded condemnation of homosexual practice. For classical commentary, we will consult a work that is usually attributed to the early companion and prolific source of traditions about Muhammad's life, Abdullah Ibn Abbas, whom we encountered earlier. It was compiled by the medieval theologian Abu al-Tahir Muhammad al-Shirazi al-Firuzabadi (d. 1414 CE). This work comments on the key verses 165–166 as follows: "What! Of all creatures (do ye come unto the males) for sexual intercourse, (And leave the wives) and avoid having sex with your wives (your Lord created for you) that your Lord made lawful for you? (Nay, but ye are forward folk)

---

10. Qutb, *In the Shade*, 6:116–17 (emphasis added).

who transgress from the lawful to the unlawful."[11] Moving to the modern era, we again consider the Egyptian scholar and activist Sayyid Qutb. His commentary on this particular pericope is consistent with his previous response discussed above:

> Lot's people, who inhabited several villages in the Jordan Valley, were known for their sinful practice of homosexuality, which reflects a *wicked perversion* of human nature. God has created human males and females, making each sex naturally inclined to the other in order for human life to progress through procreation. This mutual inclination is, then, part of the universal law that ensures balance and harmony among all creatures in the universe, whether animate or inanimate, and makes them cooperate in the fulfilment of God's will that governs the entire universe. When a man has sex with another man, their practice neither fulfils any objective nor serves the nature of the universe and its laws. It is indeed singular that anyone should find pleasure in such a practice. The pleasure a man finds with a woman is indeed the means through which human nature fulfils God's will. Thus, the *deviation from natural law* is clear in Lot's people's actions. Hence, it was inevitable that they should refrain from their deviation or be destroyed.[12]

There are clear resonances between this statement by Sayyid Qutb and the commentary by Abul A'la Maududi on Q7:80–84 cited above. Is there any reference in the sacred texts of Islam that can be seen to allude to acceptable homosexual activity? Some scholars answer in the affirmative, suggesting that verses such as Q52:24, Q56:17, and Q76:19 referring to believers being served by youths in paradise refer to homosexual relations.[13] However, these Qur'anic references merely suggest that the youths circulate (*yatufu*) amongst the believers, without any explicit sexual reference. To read a subtext of homosexual activity would be forced, in the absence of further evidence.

The Hadith

The Hadith, or prophetic traditions, that Muslims consider to record the statements and deeds of Muhammad, Messenger of Islam, contain a

---

11. Al-Firuzabadi, *Tanwir al-Miqbas*, 420.
12. Sayyid Qutb, *In the Shade*, 13:61 (emphasis added).
13. Bosworth, "Liwat," 5:778.

PART II: ENGAGING ETHICALLY WITH WIDER SOCIETY

number of references to homosexuals. Consider the following report taken from the authoritative Sunni collection of Abu Dawud: "Narrated Abdullah ibn Abbas: The Prophet (peace_be_upon_him) said: If you find anyone doing as Lot's people did, kill the one who does it, and the one to whom it is done."[14] In this Hadith report, Abdullah ibn Abbas (d. 687 CE), a younger contemporary and companion of Muhammad, relates that the Messenger of Islam urged that anyone "doing as Lot's people did" should be executed. There are other references in the Hadith collections to the people of Lot. The following report was taken from another Sunni collection, assembled by the ninth-century scholar al-Tirmidhi: "Narrated Jabir: That the Messenger of Allah (peace_be_upon_him) said: 'What I fear most from my Ummah is the behaviour of the people of Lot.'"[15] Although some scholars question the authenticity of this particular tradition, it nevertheless occurs in the major collections and reinforces the perception of the people of Lot as pursuing undesirable behavior.

A further point of reference to the people of Lot is found in the collection of the *Stories of the Prophets* assembled by the medieval theologian Ibn Kathir (d. 1373 CE). In this work, Ibn Kathir devotes several chapters to prophetic figures from the Islamic tradition, including the figure of Lot. In this account, Lot visits the city of Sodom and is distressed by what he finds:

> This city was filled with evil. Its residents waylaid, robbed and killed travelers. Another common evil among them was that men had sex with men instead of with women. This unnatural act later became known as sodomy (after the city of Sodom). It was practiced openly and unashamedly. It was at the height of these crimes and sins that Allah revealed to Prophet Lot (PBUH) that he should summon the people to give up their indecent behavior, but they were so deeply sunk in their immoral habits that they were deaf to Lot's preaching. Swamped in their unnatural desires, they refused to listen, even when Lot warned them of Allah's punishment. Instead, they threatened to drive him out of the city if he kept on preaching. . . . The doings of Lot's people saddened his heart. Their unwholesome reputation spread throughout the land, while he struggled against them. As the years passed, he persisted in his mission but to no avail. No one responded to his call and believed except for the members of his family, and even

---

14. Owner of Site, "Prescribed Punishments"; van der Krogt, "Friday Essay."
15. Owner of Site, "The Book on Legal Punishments."

in his household, not all the members believed. Lot's wife, like Noah's wife, was a disbeliever.[16]

In this account, Lot persists against all odds in trying to persuade the people of Sodom to renounce their evil ways. He endures ridicule and violence. "He urged them to seek sexual fulfillment with their wives, for that is what Allah had made lawful. Lot's people waited until he had finished his short sermon, and then they roared with laughter."[17] Eventually Lot himself despairs of ever persuading the people of Sodom to change their ways. He calls on God to destroy the city and punishment follows swiftly:

> The angels warned Prophet Lot (PBUH) to leave his house before sunrise, taking with him all his family except his wife. Allah had decreed that the city of Sodom should perish. An earthquake rocked the town. It was as if a mighty power had lifted the entire city and flung it down in one jolt. A storm of stones rained on the city. Everyone and everything was destroyed, including Lot's wife.[18]

So in both the Hadith accounts and the *Stories of the Prophets* Lot is vindicated while those of his people who engage in homosexual activity stand condemned. Such materials gained wide distribution and exerted a powerful influence in shaping Muslim attitudes down the ages. So a label commonly attached to homosexuals is "Lot's people"; even if Muslim individuals do not use the label themselves, its negative reference to homosexuals is widely understood.

Other Relevant References

Beyond specific references to the people of Lot, other negative references to homosexuality abound in the Islamic primary texts. Consider the following further report in the Hadith collection of Abu Dawud which makes no mention of Lot and his people: "Narrated Abdullah ibn Abbas: If a man who is not married is seized committing sodomy, he will be stoned to death."[19] Similarly, the famous collection of Hadith by the great jurist Imam Malik, entitled the *Muwatta'*, confirmed the gruesome death sentence laid down for sodomy in Hadith no. 1530: "Malik reported

---

16. Ibn Kathir, *Stories of the Prophets*.
17. Ibn Kathir, *Stories of the Prophets*.
18. Ibn Kathir, *Stories of the Prophets*.
19. "Sunan Abu-Dawud."

PART II: ENGAGING ETHICALLY WITH WIDER SOCIETY

that he asked Ibn Shihab what the order was regarding a man committing sodomy. Ibn Shihab said that he should be stoned whether he be married or unmarried."[20] The primary sources are unambiguous about the view of homosexual activity laid down in some of the primary textual material. While the *Stories of the Prophets* make no claim to sacred text status, they provide the foundations for much popular storytelling that has circulated throughout Islamic societies down the centuries. By contrast, the Hadith collections do make a claim to being part of Islam's sacred corpus. In summary, the weight of evidence drawn from the primary texts of Islam—Qur'an, Hadith, Tafsir—based on the above representative sample, points to a strong condemnation of homosexual activity underpinning textual Islam. But what about in practice? How has Islam dealt with this? With this conclusion, we can now move on to consider homosexual practice within Islamic communities down the centuries.

The Earliest Period: 632–780 CE

In most societies throughout history homosexuality appears to have been practiced, at least by some individuals. There is no written evidence of homosexuality during the first 150 years of Islam, i.e., the period 632 to 780 CE. It is unlikely that it was nonexistent, because homosexuality was practiced among the pre-Islamic Arabs. One researcher reports that "the Quraysh tribe, to which Muhammad belonged, included many passive homosexuals—so numerous that they were proverbial."[21] The Islamic written sources from this period are relatively scarce, so homosexuality may have been practiced but simply underreported. If indeed homosexuality was not widely exhibited in this first 150 years of Islam, several ideas have been put forward to explain this: First, the punishment for sodomy practiced by the first Muslims may have been so harsh and rigidly applied that it served as an effective deterrent. Second, it is possible that homosexuality was present among the initial Muslims but not reported because it was considered too shameful to be discussed.[22] However, homosexual activity within the

20. Malik, *Muwatta*.
21. Daniel, "Arab Civilization," 60.
22. There is a parallel in the censorship applied by the commentator Ibn Hisham (d. 833 CE). In his recension of Ibn Ishaq's *Sirat Rasul Allah* (Biography of the Prophet of Allah), he admits that "[Also left out are] verses which he [Ibn Ishaq] mentioned but none of the connoisseurs of poetry I met was acquainted with, things that are either

Islamic community has been widely described by Muslim writers in many times and places after that. Since the shame issue did not seem to apply universally in other times, why should that early era be an exception? Third, it has been suggested that male homosexual activity was a response to the shortage of available women.[23] In the first century and a half of Islam, there was a surplus of women for sexual contact due to the Islamic conquests of the surrounding countries. Female captives were freely distributed to the Muslim troops and used for sexual purposes.[24] The Qur'an describes "those who your right hand possesses" (*ma malakat aymanakum*)[25] as women upon whom a Muslim man may enforce his sexual desires. Abdul Hamid Siddiqui, distinguished Fellow of the Islamic Research Academy of Karachi, and translator of the *Sahih Muslim* Hadith collection, states: "the expression *malakat aymanukum* (those whom your right hands possess) [in Q.4:24] denotes slave-girls i.e., women who were captured in the Holy War. When women are taken captive their previous marriages are automatically annulled ... [and] sexual intercourse with these women is lawful with certain conditions."[26] A chapter in *Sahih Muslim* outlines these conditions. It is entitled: "It is permissible to have intercourse with a female captive after it is established that she is not pregnant, and if she has a husband then her marriage is annulled when she is captured." This is based on an event in the life of Muhammad, describing the occasion when the Qur'anic verse Q4:24 was revealed: "[O]n the Day of Hunain, the Messenger of Allah sent an army to Awtâs, where they met the enemy, fought them and prevailed over them. They captured some female prisoners, and it was as if the Companions of the Messenger of Allah felt reluctant to have intercourse with them because of their idolater husbands. Then Allah, the Mighty and Sublime, revealed: 'Also (forbidden are) women already married, except those (slaves) whom your right hands possess,' meaning, they are permissible for you once their 'Iddah has ended."[27] The successful warfare by Muslims against non-Muslims during the lifetime of Muhammad and in the early centuries following ensured that there was a constant supply of women

---

disgraceful to talk about ... or such that may distress certain people ..." Guillaume, *Life of Muhammad*, 691.

23. Čvorović, "Islamic Homosexuality," 85–103.
24. See, for example, *Sahih alBukhari*, 8:600; 9:506.
25. Qur'an, 4:25; also 23:5, 6 and 70:29, 30.
26. *Sahih Muslim*, 2:897.
27. *Sahih Muslim*, 4:108.

captured for sexual exploitation. Goitein suggests sociological reasons for why an abundant source of women for sex might, counterintuitively, result in a growth of homosexual practice:

> It [the spread of homosexuality in pre-Islamic and early Islamic times] was the outcome of the superimposition of a caste of warlike conquerors over a vast defenseless population. The steamrollers of the Assyrian, Babylonian, Persian, Macedonian, and Roman conquests had crushed all the independent nations of the Ancient Near East. What remained was human dust, a population that was not accustomed to bearing arms and was unable to fight. Any conqueror, whether Arab, Turk, or Mongol, could take what he liked. After the endless supply of girls of all races, colors, shapes and personalities had been tasted, the oversatiated and refined appetites had to be satisfied elsewhere. Thus the cult of the ephebes, or attractive male youths, originally was a privilege of the men in power. But as often happens with social mores, the example of the ruling class filtered down, and became a style of life for the entire community.[28]

Finally, another explanation is that Arab Islamic culture inherited homosexuality from the societies it conquered, such as the Persians, and it took some time before this practice was taken up.[29] If that is so, this new inheritance was embraced with enthusiasm. After that early period, and throughout Islamic history, homosexuality has been widely reported and practiced in the Muslim world.

The Period 780–1000 CE

Homosexuality is documented among Muslims in the late eighth century, when the Umayyad dynasty (r. 661–750 CE) was replaced by the Abbasids, based in Baghdad (r. 750–1258 CE). The historian Abu ʿUthman ʿAmr ibn Bahr al-Kinani al-Basri (776–868 CE) was known as al-Jahiz, "the boggle-eyed," because of his unusual physiognomy. He was a prolific writer, accredited with over two hundred books, of which thirty have survived. It is claimed that he died when a pile of books from his private library fell and crushed him.[30] He suggested that the genesis of homosexuality in the

---

28. Goitein, "Sexual Mores," 47–48.
29. Khalil, "Unknown Aspect," 35.
30. Pellat, "Al-Jahiz," 81.

Muslim community arose from the Abbasid army policy of nonaccompaniment of the soldiers by their wives. As a result, young male pages were used for sexual purposes.[31] The development of paid standing armies and the growth of Islamic administration meant that all booty, including women taken as prisoners of war, now belonged to the state. This was accompanied and ameliorated somewhat by a policy of keeping local populations intact to maintain and farm the newly conquered lands for taxation purposes. These new policies may have led to a decreased military use of captured women for sexual exploitation. Khalil posits that the wider social and economic situation may have also been a factor in the new expression of homosexuality. He quotes Awadh and Gide:

> It is a mistake to believe that the periods of homosexuality in ancient times was [sic] only periods of corruption; on the contrary, they were the brightest periods in that history, like the period of Pericles the Greek, Augustus, the Roman emperor, the period of Shakespeare in Britain, the period of the Renaissance in Britain, Italy and France (under the rule for Luis, sic) 13th, and the period of Hafiz in Persia, which are periods during which homosexuality was about to become official.[32]

The eighth century is widely seen as the advent of the Golden Age of Islam, when Islamic culture and science flowered. There was new contact between different cultures—Arab, Persian, Greek, and Turkish. Khalil makes a moral judgment: "It was natural that the liberal surrounding environment and its products at that time would lead to scandalous sorts of flirtation, debauchery, and homosexuality."[33] Al-Jahiz himself is widely believed to have been a practicing homosexual. He wrote much about it, at times promoting it, and at other times opposing it. He lived through the rules of ten caliphs, including Haroun al-Rashid (r. 786–809 CE) and al-Amin (r. 809–813 CE). Homosexuality appears at the highest levels. Khalil suggests that:

> ... some Caliphs were among those who practiced homosexuality most. Some of them include: al-Amin, and previously, his father Haroun al-Rashid, who was permissive in this issue. If this was the

---

31. Trexler, *Sex and Conquest*, 52.
32. Awadh and Gide, *Corydon, Majallat al-Qahira*, 108.
33. Khalil, "Unknown Aspect," 35.

PART II: ENGAGING ETHICALLY WITH WIDER SOCIETY

condition for the elite people, what about the others? As the saying goes: people adopt the religion of their kings!³⁴

The Abbasid caliph Al-Amin (r. 809–813 CE) was openly gay. Muslim historian Al Tabari wrote that he fell madly in love with one of his male slaves, Kauthar, whom he had named after a river in paradise. In an attempt to lure her son away from his homosexuality, Al-Amin's mother required his slave girls to wear men's clothing so he could be persuaded to have sex with them. This led to the phenomenon of *ghulamiyyat*, girls who dressed and acted like boys to attract male interest from those who preferred men over women. This is reflected in the literature of the period.³⁵ Another prominent leader who openly practiced homosexuality was Abu Muslim al-Khorasani, the all-conquering Persian general who led the Abbasid army to victory over the Umayyads. When asked about the best kind of life, he proposed "delicious food, yellow wine, and a youth with deep-white-black eyes." Explaining his preference for young men over odalisques, he itemized the following: "On your way, he is a companion; when you are drinking, he is a drinking companion; and when you are alone, he is a wife."³⁶ The poet Abu Nawas (756–814 CE) was based at the Abbasid court in Baghdad and he wrote many homoerotic poems. *In the Bath-House* serves as one example:

> In the bath-house, the mysteries hidden by trousers
> Are revealed to you.
> All becomes radiantly manifest.
> Feast your eyes without restraint!
> You see handsome buttocks, shapely trim torsos,
> You hear the guys whispering pious formulas
> to one another
> ("God is Great!" "Praise be to God!")
> Ah, what a palace of pleasure is the bath-house!
> Even when the towel-bearers come in
> And spoil the fun a bit.³⁷

Other poets who openly practiced and promoted homosexuality in the Abbasid court included Bashar bin Burd (714–784 CE), Muti' bin Iyas (704–785 CE), Yahya bin Ziyad (774–847 CE), Hammad Ajrad (b. 714 CE), Salm b. 'Amr al-Khasir (d. 802 CE), Waliba bin al-Habbab (late ninth century),

---

34. Khalil, "Unknown Aspect," 35.
35. Bosworth, "Liwat," 5:777.
36. Bakkar, *Ittijahat al-Ghazal*, 185.
37. "In the Bath-House: Poem by Abu Nuwas."

and Aban al-Lahiqi (c. 750–815 CE).[38] Homosexual practice was not limited to creative artists. Other public figures included grammarians such as Abu Obaydah from Basra, the widely reported transmitter of the Qur'an Ali bin Hamzah al Kisa'i,[39] the judges Yahya bin Aktham[40] and al-Juranji, and the minister and author al Sahib bin Abbad.[41] Poems were recited deriding the public hypocrisy in this matter: "Our emir is bribed; our ruler practices homosexuality, evil spreads among the people; a judge forces the law on fornicators but does not force it on homosexuals."[42] The practice is widely reported across the succeeding eras and was geographically spread. The Aghlabid Ibrahim II was the Emir of Ifriqiya, which consisted of Tunisia and Sicily. He ruled from 875 to 902 CE. He was said to have been surrounded by some sixty catamites or young male sex workers, whom he treated, as he did most other people, quite brutally.[43] In Cordoba, Spain, the Andalusian Caliph Abdul Rahman III reigned from 912 to 961 CE. He was well known as a pederast. He is reported as killing a young Christian male hostage who refused his sexual advances.[44] But homosexual activity by Muslim leaders was about more than just sex. Homosexual positions were seen as an expression of power relations. The top partner or "pointer" is considered hypermasculine, a dominant role to be proud of, whereas the "receiver" is viewed as shamefully and submissively feminine.

From 1000 CE to the Modern Period

Sultan Mahmud of Ghazni (971–1030 CE) was the Islamic conqueror of Eastern Iran, Afghanistan, and Pakistan. He was well known for his affair with his Turkish slave Malik Ayaz.[45] In this case, the slave was the "pointer" and the sultan was the "receiver." Sufi poets used it to illustrate the power of love, pointing to Mahmud as an example of a man who becomes "a slave to his slave," while Malik Ayaz served as "the embodiment of the ideal beloved,

---

38. Schmitt and Sofer, *Sexuality and Eroticism*, 13–19.

39. Bakkar, *Ittijahat al-Ghazal*, 189–90; Mahmoud and al-Mahthoorah, *Al-Shuthuth al-Jinsi*, 168–227.

40. Al-Sharishi, *Sharh Maqamat al-Hariri al-Busayri*, 1:185.

41. Al-Jahiz, *Rasael*, 2:195; Rosenthal, "Male and Female," 28.

42. Al-Sharishi, *Sharh Maqamat al-Hariri al-Busayri*, 1:185–86.

43. Bosworth, "Liwat," 5:777.

44. Bosworth, "Liwat," 5:777.

45. Owner of site, "Historical Look at Attitudes."

PART II: ENGAGING ETHICALLY WITH WIDER SOCIETY

and a model for purity in Sufi literature." In one poem a box of pearls is broken open spilling out its contents. All the other men run to grab some booty, but Malik stays behind Mahmud, stating that the sultan is sufficient for him. Mahmud then makes Malik the king of Lahore.[46] Jalaludin Rumi (1207–1273) is probably Islam's most famous poet. For months he locked himself in a room with an older man Shams Tabrizi (1185–1248), a vagrant. The close connection between the two men was a scandal in their time, and many suspected them of sodomy. However other Muslim writers have denied that there was any sexual element in their relationship.[47]

In the Punjab during the sixteenth century a Sufi saint and poet Shah Hussain was greatly admired. His poems of love are still recited and sung in many parts of the world. A very public love relationship between him and Madho Lal, a Hindu Brahman boy, developed. They lived together, died, and are buried side by side in the same tomb in Lahore.[48] The Indian Mughal Emperor Babur (1483–1530) admitted in his autobiography his attraction to a boy in the camp bazaar. This was a celebrated work of literature in the medieval Muslim world.[49] In the eighteenth century, Dargah Quli Khan, a nobleman from the Deccan traveling to Delhi, wrote about how widespread homosexuality had become in Indo-Islamic society. Male prostitutes solicited openly in the public bazaars, and Khan wrote that "young good-looking men danced everywhere and created great excitement."[50] Sufism spoke much of love, and homosexual relationships were, throughout Islamic history, considered to be a legitimate expression of that love. There are many illustrated manuals from the seventeenth to the nineteenth centuries depicting explicitly homosexual and heterosexual acts, including group sex.[51]

Because of its widespread practice, the Turkish Ottoman Empire decriminalized homosexuality in 1858.[52] The openly gay British poet Lord Byron traveled to Turkey in the nineteenth century due to the more tolerant attitude towards homosexuality that existed in the Ottoman Empire,

---

46. Owner of site, "Homosexual Icon."
47. Cherry, "Rumi: Poet and Sufi Mystic."
48. Warriach, "Love Needs No Guidance."
49. Owner of Site, "Historical Look at Attitudes."
50. Daniyel, "Orlando Shooting."
51. Pinkstone, "From Sex on a Grave."
52. Owner of Site, "Historical Look at Attitudes."

allowing him to carry out his desires with young men.[53] It is probable that Western colonialism contributed to a change. In 1860 the British promulgated the Indian Penal Code, which included section 377 outlawing homosexuality. This law, despite its various iterations, continues in modern-day India, Pakistan, and Bangladesh.[54] In this way the conservative mores of Victorian culture were imposed upon a previously homophilic society. Shoaib Daniyal notes that today the only five Muslim countries where homosexual activity is not a crime (Mali, Jordan, Indonesia, Turkey, and Albania) were never colonized by the British.[55] However another movement was also taking place. In Arabia, the preacher and activist, Muhammad ibn Abd al-Wahhab (1703–1792) formed an alliance with a local ruler named Muhammad bin Saud. The resulting House of Saud continued to expand its territory but did not have a major international influence until 1932 when the Kingdom of Saudi Arabia was formed and oil was discovered in 1938. They called on Islam to return to the Qur'an and the practice of the prophet Muhammad. Since that time the Wahhabis have been exporting their brand of conservative Islam everywhere. Among their teachings is the prohibition of homosexuality.[56] They have, in a sense, completed the historical circle, making the original Islamic proscription of homosexuality mainstream.

The Modern Period

The modern scene with regards to homosexuality can be represented as six points on a spectrum which are in conflict with each other. Some Muslims and Islamic states advocate the death penalty, following the dictates of the Qur'an and the Hadith. Others openly or privately state their disagreement with the practice, while a few completely deny its existence within Islam. Some tacitly condone it, if done in private, due to a live and let live attitude. Others practice it secretly, and increasingly there are some who openly and even stridently advocate for the gay lifestyle. Muslims typically do not like to talk about this topic openly and are somewhat embarrassed by it. We will look at examples of each of these views. At the radical end of the spectrum

---

53. MacCarthy, "Poet of All the Passions."

54. Though India is in the process of change as on 6 September 2018 the Supreme Court of India declared section 377 of the Indian Penal Code unconstitutional.

55. Daniyal, "Orlando Shooting."

56. Vallely, "Wahhabism: A Deadly Scripture."

PART II: ENGAGING ETHICALLY WITH WIDER SOCIETY

is the total repudiation of homosexuality as acceptable for Muslims, or anyone else. This finds its expression in fundamentalist groups like ISIS, where homosexuals are thrown off buildings, or in the Taliban, where they are crushed under collapsed walls. It can also be found in state-sponsored punishments. In its 1991 Constitution, in Articles 108–113, Iran mandated the punishment of execution for sodomy. It is estimated that between four thousand to six thousand gay people have been executed in Iran since the revolution of 1979.[57] In northern Nigeria, where Sharia law governs twelve Muslim-majority states, homosexuality attracts capital punishment by stoning.[58] In April 2005 in Saudi Arabia, 105 men were sentenced for acts of "deviant sexual behavior" following their March arrests. It was claimed they illegally danced together and were "behaving like women." Seventy men received one-year prison sentences while thirty-one got six months to one year, plus two hundred lashes each. Four others faced two years behind bars plus two thousand lashes.[59]

Anti-homosexual laws can be used against others. A famous example was Anwar Ibrahim, the Malaysian politician who was imprisoned twice on sodomy charges which are now officially admitted to be "a miscarriage of justice."[60] In 2001, the Egyptian Ministry of Culture, under pressure from Islamic fundamentalists, burnt six thousand volumes of eighth-century poet Abu Nuwas's homoerotic verses.[61] Some Muslim organizations and individuals oppose homosexuality but do not argue that coercion should be used to prevent it. During the recent Australian gay marriage debate, the statement from the National Imams Council was clear: "Islam . . . explicitly and unambiguously states that marital relationship is only permissible between a man and woman; any other marital relationships are Islamicly (sic) impermissible."[62] However, they did not propose any punishment or sanctions against those who engaged in such activity. Some Muslims deny that homosexuality exists in their countries. In 2007, at Columbia University, Iranian President Mahmoud Ahmadinejad claimed: "In Iran we don't have homosexuals like in your country. I do not know who

---

57. Boteach, "Gay Marriage Problem."
58. Murdock, "Gays in the Islamic World."
59. Murdock, "Gays in the Islamic World."
60. Chan, "Malaysia's Jailed Leader-in-Waiting."
61. Mehrez, "Take Them Out."
62. Baird, "Same-Sex Marriage."

ISLAM AND HOMOSEXUALITY

has told you we have it."[63] Some in the center of the spectrum are those holding a tolerant definition of who is a Muslim. The Egyptian-Swiss scholar, Professor Tariq Ramadan states that:

> "homosexuality is forbidden in Islam, but . . . we must avoid condemning or rejecting individuals. It is quite possible to disagree with a person's behaviour (public or private), while respecting that person as an individual. . . . [A] person who pronounces the attestation of Islamic faith becomes a Muslim; if that person engages in homosexual practices, no one has the right to drive him or her out of Islam. Behaviour considered reprehensible under the rules of morality cannot justify excommunication."[64]

Further along the spectrum would be those who practice homosexual acts but attempt to keep it secret. These include predatory acts on younger vulnerable people. Pedophilia involving boys is widely practiced in the madrassas of Pakistan, according to a recent report.[65] And in neighboring Afghanistan, British troops were scandalized by the cultural practice of "bacha bazi" where young boys are dressed up as girls and made to dance before being used for sex by older men.[66] For others homosexual activity is freely chosen. Saudi Arabia, for example, has a thriving underground gay culture, for both males and females. Yasser, a twenty-six-year-old artist, in Jeddah said: "It's a lot easier to be gay than straight here. If you go out with a girl, people will start to ask her questions. But if I have a [male] date upstairs and my family is downstairs, they won't even come up."[67] At the far end of the spectrum are those who openly practice and publicly advocate homosexuality. These include gay imams in the US and the UK and now in Australia who lead homophilic congregations. In Melbourne, Somali-born Imam Nur Warsame is planning to establish Australia's first gay-friendly mosque. He noted the plight of other homosexual Muslims, under threat because of their gay lifestyle. *"I had seven people housed at my one-bedroom apartment . . . because it was life or death for them. They had to leave [their homes] that day, then and there."*[68]

---

63. Markoe, "Muslim Attitudes about LGBT."
64. Ramadan, "Islam and Homosexuality."
65. Owner of Site, "Pakistan's Hidden Shame."
66. Palin, "Bacha Bazi."
67. Labi, "The Kingdom in the Closet."
68. Owner of Site, "How Have Muslims Reacted."

Some Muslim scholars are trying to develop an Islamic theology which allows for and even endorses homosexual practice. Scott Siraj al-Haqq Kugle has written two books to present homosexuality in a positive light in contrast to previous negative views held by Islamic scholars.[69] He argues that the early texts attacked not homosexual love but lust in all its forms. He concludes:

> At the end of the day, many Muslims will respond that it is too much for lesbian and gay Muslims to ask for Islam to change to accommodate them. However, this is not really what we are asking for. In reality, we assert that Islam must change to grow, to continue growing as it had in the past, confident that in facing new challenges with a keen sense of justice Muslims will renew the roots of their faith. Lesbian, transgender, and gay Muslims assert that we may be agents in this slow but necessary change, along with women, youth, and other disempowered groups.[70]

Conclusion

It has been seen that the earliest Islamic texts and their interpretation by most Muslim scholars have presented a seriously adverse view of homosexuality. The usual judicial punishment prescribed has been execution. However, it is also clear that, throughout history, homosexuality has been widely practiced in the Muslim world, even at the highest political and social levels. Disobedience to the legal precepts has characterized every age of Muslim history. In recent years there has been a harsh response to homosexuality from the Wahhabi version of Islam promoted by Saudi Arabia. Today the wide range of views on homosexuality held and lived out by some Muslims is in stark contrast to the singular and consistent condemnation of it found in the texts and scholarly judgments. More recent scholarship has begun to challenge the traditional views. With respect to homosexuality, Islam faces a significant challenge reconciling the stringent demands of its law with the expressed desires and practices of some of its adherents.

---

69. Kugle, *Homosexuality in Islam*; Kugle, *Living out Islam*.
70. Kugle, *Homosexuality in Islam*, 273.

Bibliography

Al-Fīrūzabādī, Muḥammad. *Tanwīr al-Miqbās min Tafsīr Ibn 'Abbās*. Translated by Mokrane Guezzou. Amman: Royal Aal al-Bayt Institute for Islamic Thought, 2007.

Al-Hilali, Muhammad Taqi-ud-Din al-Hilali, and Muhammad Muhsin Khan. *Translation of the Meanings of The Noble Qur'an in the English Language*. Madinah: King Fahd Complex, 2000.

Al-Mahalli, Jalal al-Din, and Jalal al-Din al-Suyuti. *Tafsir al-Jalalayn*. Translated by F. Hamza. Amman: Royal Aal al-Bayt Institute for Islamic Thought, 2007.

Al-Sharishi. *Sharh Maqamat al-Hariri al-Busayri*. Beirut: Maktabat al-Thaqafah, 2006.

Awadh, R., and Gide, Andre. *Corydon (Autobiography), Majallat al-Qahira*. Cairo: Al-Haya'at al-Missriyyah al-Aammah li al-Kuttab, no. 162, 1996.

Baird, Julia. "Same-Sex Marriage: Why Have Muslims Been So Quiet in the Debate?" *Australian Broadcasting Corporation*. Accessed September 20, 2018. http://www.abc.net.au/news/2017-08-31/same-sex-marriage-why-have-muslims-been-so-quiet-in-debate/8860486.

Bakkar, Yousof. *Ittijahat al-Ghazal fi al-Qarn al-Thani al-Hijri, al-Ghazal al-Shaz fi al-Muthakkar*. 2nd edition. Sharjah: Dar al-Andalus, n.d.

Bosworth, Clifford Edmund. "Liwat." In *Encyclopaedia of Islam*, vol. 4. Edited by C. E. Bosworth, 777–78. Leiden: Brill, 1986.

Boteach, Shmuley. "How Iran Solved Its Gay Marriage Problem." *The Observer*. Accessed September 16, 2018. https://observer.com/2015/05/how-iran-solved-its-gay-marriage-problem.

Chan, Tara Francis. "Malaysia's Jailed Leader-in-Waiting Has Been Released from Custody and Given a Full Royal Pardon." *Business Insider Malaysia*. Accessed September 16, 2018. https://www.businessinsider.my/malaysias-anwar-ibrahim-pardoned-and-released-from-jail-2018-5/?r=US&IR=T.

Cherry, Kittredge. "Rumi: Poet and Sufi Mystic Inspired by Same-Sex Love." *Qspirit*. Accessed September 15, 2018. https://qspirit.net/rumi-same-sex-love.

Cowburn, Ashley. "Isis Has Killed At Least 25 Men in Syria Suspected of Being Gay, Group Claims." *The Independent* (January 5, 2016). https://www.independent.co.uk/news/world/middle-east/isis-has-killed-at-least-25-men-in-syria-suspected-of-being-gay-group-claims-a6797636.html.

Čvorović, Jelena. "Islamic Homosexuality." *Antropologija* 1 (2006) 85–103.

Daniel, Marc. "Arab Civilization and Male Love," trans. Winston Leyland, in *Reclaiming Sodom*, ed. Jonathan Goldberg (New York: Routledge, 1994).

Daniyal, Shoaib. "Orlando Shooting: It's Different Now, But Muslims Have a Long History of Accepting Homosexuality." *Scroll-In*. Accessed September 18, 2018. https://scroll.in/article/810093/orlando-shooting-its-different-now-but-muslims-have-a-long-history-of-accepting-homosexuality.

Durie, Mark. *The Third Choice*. Melbourne: Deror, 2010.

Guillaume, Alfred. *The Life of Muhammad: A Translation of Ibn Ishaq's Sirat Rasul Allah*. Oxford: Oxford University Press, 1955.

Goitein, Shelomo. "The Sexual Mores of the Common People." In *Society and the Sexes in Medieval Islam*, edited by AfafLutfi al-Sayyid-Marsot. Malibu: Undena Publications, 1979.

Ibn Kathir, Imaduddin Abul-Fida Ismail. *Stories of the Prophets*. Riyadh: Darussalam, 1996.

PART II: ENGAGING ETHICALLY WITH WIDER SOCIETY

"Istanbul Pride." Wikipedia. Accessed August 13, 2018. https://en.wikipedia.org/wiki/Istanbul_Pride.

Khalil, Mohammad. "An Unknown Aspect in the Life of Al-Jahiz." *Al-Qasemi Magazine*, vol. 1 (2009). http://www.medievalists.net/2011/10/an-unknown-aspect-in-the-life-of-al-jahiz/.

Kugle, Scott Siraj al-Haqq. *Homosexuality in Islam: Critical Reflections on Gay, Lesbian and Transgender Muslims*. Oxford: OneWorld Publications, 2010.

Kugle, Scott Siraj al-Haqq. *Living out Islam: Voices of Gay, Lesbian and Transgender Muslims*. New York: New York University Press, 2015.

Labi, Nadya. "The Kingdom in the Closet." *The Atlantic* (May 2007). https://www.theatlantic.com/magazine/archive/2007/05/the-kingdom-in-the-closet/305774/.

MacCarthy, Fiona. "Poet of All the Passions." *The Guardian*. Accessed September 15, 2018. https://www.theguardian.com/books/2002/nov/09/classics.poetry.

Malik, Imam. *Muwatta*. Translated by Muhammad Rahimuddin. 4th edition. New Delhi: Kitab Bhavan, 1992.

Markoe, Lauren. "Muslim Attitudes about LGBT Are Complex, Far from Universally Anti-gay." *USA Today*. Accessed September 20, 2018. https://www.usatoday.com/story/news/world/2016/06/17/muslim-lgbt-gay-views/86046404.

Maududi, Sayyid Abul Ala. *Tafhim al-Qur'an—The Meaning of the Qur'an*. Accessed August 13, 2018. http://www.englishtafsir.com/Quran/7/index.html#sdfootnote64sym.

Mehrez, Samia. "Take Them Out of the Ballgame: Egypt's Cultural Players in Crisis." *Middle East Report* 219 (2001). Accessed September 20, 2018. https://www.merip.org/mer/mer219/take-them-out-ballgame#_6.

Murdock, Deroy. "Gays in the Islamic World." *Cato Institute*. Accessed September 16, 2018. https://www.cato.org/publications/commentary/gays-islamic-world.

Owner of Site. "The Book on Legal Punishments (Al-Hudud)." *Jami' at-Tirmidhi*. Accessed August 13, 2018. https://sunnah.com/search/?q=%22people+of+Lot%22.

Owner of Site. "A Historical Look at Attitudes to Homosexuality in the Islamic World." Accessed September 15, 2018. https://libcom.org/history/historical-look-attitudes-homosexuality-islamic-world.

Owner of Site. "How Have Muslims Reacted to a LGBT-Friendly Mosque in Australia Run by a Gay Imam?" *Al-Bawaba*. Accessed September 15, 2018. https://www.albawaba.com/loop/how-have-muslims-reacted-lgbt-friendly-mosque-australia-run-gay-imam-1165844.

Owner of Site. "Pakistan's Hidden Shame: Documentary Reveals Horrors of Pedophilia in KP." *Dawn*. Accessed September 20, 2018. https://www.dawn.com/news/1129614.

Owner of Site. "Prescribed Punishments (Kitab Al-Hudud)." *Sunan Abi Dawud*. Accessed August 13, 2018. https://sunnah.com/search/?q=%22Lot%27s+people%22.

Palin, Megan. "Bacha Bazi: Young Boys Forced to Dress As Women and Dance Before Being Sexually Abused by Rich Men." *News*. Accessed September 20, 2018. https://www.news.com.au/lifestyle/real-life/true-stories/bacha-bazi-young-boys-forced-to-dress-as-women-and-dance-before-being-sexually-abused-by-rich-men/news-story/dd5e572e9a9fe7dd4cd54032d8b31122.

Pellat, Charles. "Al-Jahiz." In *Abbasid Belles Lettres*, edited by Julia Ashtiany et al. Cambridge, UK: Cambridge University Press, 1990.

Pinkstone, Joe. "From Sex on a Grave to Wild Orgies." *Mail Online*. Accessed September 15, 2018. http://www.dailymail.co.uk/sciencetech/article-5593699/200-year-old-sex-manual-Ottoman-Empire-goes-sale-350-000.html.

Qutb, Sayyid. *In the Shade of the Qur'an*. Markfield, UK: Islamic Foundation, 2015.

Ramadan, Tariq. "Islam and Homosexuality." Accessed September 20, 2018. https://tariqramadan.com/english/islam-and-homosexuality/.

Rosenthal, Franz. "Male and Female: Described and Compared." In *Male and Female, Homoeroticism in Classical Arabic Literature*, edited by J. W. Wright Jr. and Everett K. Rowson. New York: Columbia University Press, 1997.

Sahih Muslim (7 vols.). Translated by Nasiruddin al-Khattab. Riyadh: Maktaba Dar-us-Salam, 2007.

Schmitt, Arno, and Jehoeda Sofer. *Sexuality and Eroticism among Males in Moslem Societies*. New York: Routledge, 1991.

Trexler, R. C. *Sex and Conquest: Gender Violence, Political Order, and the European Conquest of the Americas*. Ithaca, NY: Cornell University Press, 1995.

Vallely, Paul. "Wahhabism: A Deadly Scripture." *The Independent*. Accessed September 15, 2018. https://www.independent.co.uk/news/uk/home-news/wahhabism-a-deadly-scripture-398516.html.

Van der Krogt, Christopher. "Friday Essay: The Qur'an, the Bible and Homosexuality in Islam." *The Conversation* (June 17, 2016). https://theconversation.com/friday-essay-the-quran-the-bible-and-homosexuality-in-islam-61012.

Warriach, Sameer Shafi. "Love Needs No Guidance: How Shah Hussain and Madhu Laal Defied Social Norms Past and Present." *Dawn*. Accessed October 5, 2018. https://www.dawn.com/news/1403596.

Whitaker, Brian. "Everything You Need to Know about Being Gay in Muslim Countries." *The Guardian* (June 21, 2016). https://www.theguardian.com/world/2016/jun/21/gay-lgbt-muslim-countries-middle-east.

7

Living with "Assisted Dying"

An Introduction to the Issues and Ethics of Voluntary Euthanasia and Assisted Suicide in Australia

Denise Cooper-Clarke

Introduction

Euthanasia and physician-assisted suicide (now often combined under the term "assisted dying") have been contentious issues for the last fifty years, with many attempts to legalize one or both of them in various jurisdictions in Australia and overseas. In June 2016 the much anticipated report of the Legal and Social Issues Committee Inquiry into End of Life Choices was tabled in the Victorian Parliament. It made forty-nine recommendations, twentynine of which related to palliative care, and a further nineteen to advance care planning.[1] But the most controversial and the one that received all the media attention was recommendation forty-nine, concerning so called "assisted dying": "That the Victorian Government introduce a legal framework providing for assisted dying, by enacting legislation based on the assisted dying framework outlined in this Report." Discussion of this final recommendation takes up about a quarter of the more than four-hundred-page report. The fact that forty-eight of the recommendations had nothing to do with "assisted dying" but with other issues at the end of life indicates that

1. Parliament of Victoria, *Inquiry into End of Life Choices.*

there are many things to consider when we think about dying. Euthanasia is not perhaps even the most important—every one of us will die, and only a very few ask for euthanasia—but certainly it is the most contested area. The recommendations of the report around palliative care include: the development of adequate funding; integration of palliative care into other health services; increasing access to palliative care services in regional and remote communities, residential aged care facilities, and Aboriginal communities; increased funding for community palliative care so that more patients can die at home rather than in hospital, if they wish to; the incorporation of a palliative care curriculum in medical and allied health education; and the development of guidelines for continuous palliative sedation.[2] The report also recommended the enactment in legislation of the common law relating to both the permissibility of doctors withholding and/or withdrawing futile treatment and to the principle of double effect.[3]

Killing and "Letting Die"

There is a long tradition in common morality, moral philosophy, and medicine of making a distinction between killing and "letting die." The Hippocratic tradition proscribed the administration of a lethal substance to a patient while advising physicians to refrain from intervening in clearly terminal cases.[4] The Hippocratic work, *The Art*, defines the goals of medicine as "to do away with the sufferings of the sick, to lessen the violence of their diseases, and to refuse to treat those who are overmastered by their diseases, realizing that in such cases medicine is powerless."[5] The medical profession continues to maintain a clear distinction between "letting die" in such situations and killing a patient with a lethal injection or assisting their suicide by providing a prescription for a lethal drug,[6] despite the claim by prominent and influential voices in bioethics today that the distinction, at least in some contexts, is confused and mistaken.[7] Current law in Victoria (the

---

2. Parliament of Victoria, *Inquiry into End of Life Choices*, xxix–xxxii.
3. Parliament of Victoria, *Inquiry into End of Life Choices*, xxxii.
4. Hippocrates, "The Oath," 300.
5. Hippocrates, "The Art," 193.
6. See, for example, Australian Medical Association, *Position Statement Euthanasia and Physician Assisted Suicide* (2016); American Medical Association, *Code of Medical Ethics* (2018), opinions E-5.3, 5.7 and 5.8.
7. See, for example, Rachels, "Active and Passive Euthanasia," 78–80; Beauchamp

Victorian *Medical Treatment Act* 1998) protects a competent patient's right to refuse unwanted medical treatment. In addition, doctors may withhold or withdraw treatment that is futile or unnecessarily burdensome. A number of landmark international cases have clarified that even life-prolonging treatments such as the provision of artificial ventilation or artificial nutrition and hydration (ANH, also sometimes called tube feeding) to seriously brain-damaged individuals may be discontinued at the request of family members. In Victoria, the judgment in *Gardner; re BWV [2003] VSC 173* gave permission for the Public Advocate, who was the appointed guardian of a patient with advanced dementia, to refuse ANH on her behalf. Sometimes there is uncertainty on the part of doctors, patients and/or relatives agreeing to treatment on behalf of patients as to whether the administration of pain-relieving drugs might also shorten the patient's life. Traditionally, the principle of double effect (PDE) is used to justify the use of symptom-relieving medication that might be foreseen, but is not intended, to shorten the patient's life. This means that "it can be morally good to shorten a patient's life as a foreseen and accepted but unintended side effect of an action undertaken for a good reason, even if it is agreed that intentionally killing the patient or shortening the patient's life is wrong."[8] Legally, it is generally assumed, on the basis of the English case *R v. Cox*, that if the doctor's intention is to relieve pain rather than to end life, such treatment will be lawful, on the basis of PDE. However, this has not been tested in Australian courts, so there remains some uncertainty.

Despite the widespread view that effective pain relief necessarily hastens death, there is no evidence for this belief. In a 1997 paper, Australian palliative care physician Michael Ashby stated that the accepted palliative care practice of gradually escalating opioid doses had been used safely for at least twenty years with no evidence that it caused or hastened death.[9] Another paper affirmed that "in the majority of cases treatment of pain prolongs life rather than advances death."[10] This means that the PDE need not be invoked to justify the use of these drugs by skilled and experienced practitioners, because they simply do not have a "double effect" of causing death as well as treating pain. Effective pain relief is not a form of euthanasia.

---

and Childress, *Principles of Biomedical Ethics*, 219.

    8. Boyle, "Intentions, Christian Morality," 87–88.

    9. Ashby, "Fallacies of Death Causation," 176.

    10. Wall, "Generation of Yet Another Myth," 122.

Nevertheless, given the uncertainty in some doctors' minds, and the widespread public misapprehension that pain relief may shorten life, it is wise to clarify in Victorian law that doctors may use medically accepted, appropriate, and effective pain relief at the end of life without fearing prosecution, if their intention is clearly to relieve pain and not to end life. Further, all medical practitioners should be adequately trained in the administration of pain relief at the end of life, so that no patient suffers pain unnecessarily because of lack of training of their doctor and unfounded anxieties about giving adequate pain relief.

Following the recommendation of the End of Life Choices Inquiry, legislation to allow "voluntary assisted dying" was passed in Victoria in November 2017, though it will not come into effect until 2019. Similar legislation may well be passed in other Australian states and territories in the coming years.

Voluntary Assisted Dying

When considering whether we might approve this legislation, it is important to be clear exactly what question we are addressing. First, what is "voluntary assisted dying"? The term is a euphemism. Most of us would wish to be assisted as we are dying, but this is not the same as being assisted to die. "Assisted dying" as defined in the Victorian legislation (and increasingly this is how the term is used) means either a doctor on request prescribing a lethal drug for a patient to take in order to end their life—what has always been called physician-assisted suicide (PAS)—or, if the patient is physically unable to take the drug, the doctor administering it, most likely by intravenous injection, which has always been called (active) voluntary euthanasia.[11]

We should also be clear that the question is not whether, in some extreme circumstances, one might ever be justified in ending a patient's life in order to end their suffering. Rather, it is whether legalizing this is wise social policy. One does not need to adopt an absolutist stance against all killing (or all medical killing) to oppose it being legalized. When we consider the way that the issue was debated in Victoria, there are important lessons to be

---

11. *Voluntary Assisted Dying Act 2017* (Vic) sec. 3 defines voluntary assisted dying as "the administration of a voluntary assisted dying substance," and provides for this to occur either by means of a "self-administration" permit or a "practitioner administration" permit.

learned for Christian communities and those who wish to enter the public debate on this and other moral issues.

Christian ethics is often understood as primarily deontological or duty-based, focusing on obedience to God's commands as expressed in Scripture through both rules designed for specific circumstances and more general principles.[12] A major alternative to a deontological approach is consequentialism, the theory that the rightness or wrongness of an action is determined solely by its consequences—"the end justifies the means."[13] Although consideration of the consequences of one's actions is an element of prudence or biblical wisdom, Christian ethics has not generally been understood as consequentialist. Rather, some actions are understood as right or wrong in themselves, because of the nature of the thing that is done, apart from any consideration of consequences. In past moral debates, Christians would argue on the basis of principles or moral norms, while their opponents would often base their arguments on consequences. For example, some Christians have argued that potential great benefits cannot justify the deliberate destruction of human life in embryonic stem cell research,[14] or that it is wrong to place refugees in indefinite detention in order to protect our borders and save lives at sea.[15] They say the end does not justify the means.

Ideology Trumps Evidence

It is notable that in the recent public debate on assisted dying the situation was reversed. Christian opponents relied heavily on consequentialist arguments: the risk to the lives of the vulnerable, negative perceptions of illness and disability, the effect on suicide prevention programs of the legitimation of suicide by the medical profession and the state,[16] and the inevitability of the expansion of the criteria for assisted dying (the so-called slippery slope). Arguments on the basis of the principles of the sanctity of human life and of biblical justice were largely missing from the debate in Victoria. Proponents, on the other hand, did argue on the basis of principles, the principles of respect for individual autonomy (the "right to choose") and of the relief

12. Hill, *How and Why of Love*, 24–25.
13. Nelson, "Consequentialism," 253–54.
14. Garcia and Jochemsen, "Ethics of Stem Cell Research," 72.
15. Menzies, "Do Ends Justify the Means?"
16. Yuill, "We Cannot Have 'Zero Suicides,'" para. 6.

of suffering. The submission by the Rationalist Society to the End of Life Choices Inquiry stated, "Central to medical ethics is an understanding of patient autonomy, choice and dignity. . . . In a secular liberal democracy such as ours, the individual ought to be free to organize and conduct their life in accordance with their personal values, principles and preferences, provided they do not harm others."[17] And Andrew Denton concluded the "Di Gribble Argument" lecture with, "It is not time that we had a law for assisted dying in Australia: it is well past time. . . . When someone is suffering, how can we ask them to suffer more?"[18]

This reliance on consequentialist arguments rather than principles is understandable in terms of a loss of confidence in specifically Christian arguments in the public square, based on a perception of hostility by an aggressively secular state (and much of this is related to loss of respect for the church as a result of child sexual abuse). Also, proponents of assisted dying have quite successfully promoted the view that opposition to "assisted dying" is necessarily based on religious grounds. For example, media personality Andrew Denton blamed a "hidden theocracy at the heart of government" and the Christian lobby for blocking assisted dying laws in Australia.[19] Such a view ignores the fact that the opposition of the medical profession to assisting suicide dates back to the Hippocratic tradition, four centuries before Christ, and continues today as expressed by the thoroughly secular Australian Medical Association, and indeed medical associations worldwide.[20] Nevertheless, this view has taken hold, leading to a reluctance to use specifically Christian principles in the debate. Instead, Christian opponents of assisted dying have relied on consequentialist arguments, hoping these would gain more traction in the secular space.

Yet this strategy was unsuccessful in the Victorian Parliamentary debate. Was it because the counterargument based on the principles of respect for patient choice and the relief of suffering were more powerful? Perhaps partly. But I think what actually won the day in Parliament was something quite different, and illustrates a disturbing feature of contemporary moral discourse in Australia. What won the debate was not ethical

---

17. Rationalist Society, "Submission to Parliament," paras. 4–5.
18. Denton, "Argument for Assisted Dying," para. 109.
19. Kelly, "Andrew Denton Tells Church," para. 1.
20. Hippocrates, "The Oath"; Australian Medical Association, *Code of Medical Ethics*; American Medical Association, *Position Statement*; World Medical Association, *Resolution on Euthanasia*.

argument at all, but emotive appeals based on story after story of personal experiences with the "bad deaths" of their relatives. Emotive appeals are a substitute for ethical argument that are resorted to when we have no common ground on which to base such an argument, no shared objective basis for ethics. As Alasdair MacIntyre notes, "There seems to be no rational way of securing moral agreement in our culture."[21] The evidence from overseas of the dangers of such legislation,[22] which I think is very strong, and which in all other Australian Parliaments in the past has proved decisive in rejecting "assisted dying," last year in Victoria was airily dismissed by its proponents. Ideology trumped evidence. This raises the question of whether we should rethink our reliance on consequences rather than principles in future discussion of public moral issues, or whether we need a different approach altogether.

Underlying Moral Principles

We will consider now in more detail the moral principles involved: the sanctity of human life, justice, the alleviation of suffering, and respect for individual autonomy. We note that none of these is a specifically or exclusively Christian concern. So we ought to be able to use these principles in the public square, although they will have a different basis and possibly a different shape for Christians.

All societies and cultures have laws against murder, based on the moral belief that it is wrong to kill an innocent human being. The right to life is the most basic of human rights, and the sanctity of human life is the foundation for all human rights. It should be the basis for our thinking in areas as diverse as immigration policies, treatment of indigenous peoples, capital punishment, and the conduct of war, as well as "assisted dying."

Respect for life is not just a religious value, it is a foundational value of all societies in which reasonable people would want to live.[23] From a deontological perspective, the general wrongness of killing may be framed in a number of ways, based on the intrinsic value of human life. It can be argued that the life of each individual has an equal claim to respect based on its irreducible value,[24] or that one ought never to destroy the bearer

21. MacIntyre, *After Virtue*, 6.
22. For an excellent summary of this, see Mulino, "Minority Report," 349–405.
23. Somerville, "Respect for Human Life?," para. 16.
24. Stauch, "Causal Authorship," 240.

of human dignity, which is uncompromised by disease or dependence.[25] Oderberg claims that to kill another person, even at their request, is to commit an injustice against that person, because the right to life is inalienable, since human life is the good which is fundamental to the pursuit of all other goods, including the exercise of individual autonomy.[26] The banning of dueling and of slavery are expressions of the view that we cannot waive our right to life or freedom; we may not give permission to anyone to kill or enslave us.

The sanctity of human life is also a core Christian doctrine that derives from the Genesis 1 account of humankind being created in the image of God: the imagery is of Eden as the temple of God, but in contrast to pagan temples, there is no statue to represent the god, rather humankind is the image or *ikon* which represents God. Every human being regardless of gender, race, sexual orientation, age, or state of health, is consecrated or "set apart" by God. Thus to destroy a human life (even one's own) is a symbolic attack on God himself, and this is the basis of the prohibition of murder in Genesis 9:5–6 and in the Decalogue. In the New Testament, the incarnation of Christ and his redemptive death affirms the extraordinary value he places in each human life.

The principle of the sanctity of human life underlies the traditional Christian proscription of suicide (while acknowledging that many who attempt to take their own life do so because of mental illness or out of desperation). The euphemism "assisted dying" aims to mask the fact that euthanasia and PAS are actually forms of suicide. It is incongruous that there are moves in Australia to legalize these practices at the same time as there is so much emphasis on suicide prevention.[27] Suicide is a major social problem, and we rightly spend resources aimed at reducing the suicide rate. If euthanasia and/or PAS were legalized, we would on the one hand be promoting suicide prevention, and on the other, promoting suicide as a legitimate choice. Effectively both the state and the medical professions, both very powerful institutions, legitimize and sanitize suicide. Suicide is no less tragic when a person is old rather than young, disabled rather than "normal," or sick rather than healthy. To approve suicide for some but not others is inherently discriminatory, and indicates that some lives are considered as of less value than others.

25. Sulmasy, "Killing and Allowing to Die," 61.
26. Oderberg, "Voluntary Euthanasia and Justice," 240.
27. Victoria State Government, *Victorian Suicide Prevention Framework 2016–2025*.

The principle of the sanctity of human life thus provides a powerful basis for a general prohibition on killing. Nevertheless, as long as some exceptions to this general prohibition are allowed, such as capital punishment, warfare, or self-defense, it can be argued that euthanasia and/or physician-assisted suicide might also be examples of exceptions to the rule.

This brings us to the second principle, that of justice. From a biblical perspective, justice has a strong emphasis on advocating for and protecting the vulnerable and the powerless, which includes the elderly, the sick, and the disabled.[28] It is unjust to put at further risk those whose lives are already difficult and often devalued. It will be very difficult, if not impossible, to ascertain that a patient has not been subtly or not so subtly coerced into requesting "assisted dying." Elderly, frail, and sick patients are especially vulnerable to implied or explicit messages from relatives that they are a burden and that they would be "better off dead." It is naive to assume that people always have the best interests of their relatives at heart. Elder abuse, which includes psychological and emotional abuse and neglect, is prevalent in our society.[29] But such concerns are dismissed by assisted dying advocates like British neurosurgeon, Henry Marsh, who said, "Even if a few grannies get bullied into it, isn't that the price worth paying for all the people who could die with dignity?"[30] This is consequentialist reasoning and illustrates one of the weaknesses of consequentialism—that how we assess consequences often depends on our previous commitments. Opponents of assisted dying would say that is not a price worth paying.

Advocates of "assisted dying" claim that there is no evidence of abuse of the practice in overseas jurisdictions where it is legal, and they are confident that adequate safeguards are possible to protect the vulnerable. This claim is highly contested and many who have examined the evidence from the operation of euthanasia and assisted suicide regimes in other places have concluded that effective safeguards are not possible. There are good reasons why so many jurisdictions have abandoned attempts to legalize euthanasia or PAS.

The safeguards in this legislation are that those eligible for "assisted dying" must be over the age of eighteen; that they must have capacity to make decisions about their own medical treatment; and that they must be diagnosed with a disease, illness or medical condition that is "incurable,

---

28. See, for instance, Ps 82:3–4; Prov 31:8–9; Isa 1:17.
29. Australian Institute of Family Studies, *Elder Abuse*, para. 2.
30. Chustecka, "Renowned Neurosurgeon on Assisted Dying," para. 9.

advanced, progressive and is expected to cause death within less than 6 months" (or twelve months for patients with neurodegenerative conditions such as motor neurone disease and multiple sclerosis).[31] Suffering as a result of mental illness alone does not satisfy the eligibility criteria; a doctor must be satisfied that the patient is making a voluntary decision, free from coercion, and making a properly informed decision, and "assisted dying" cannot be accessed through advance care planning.

However, there is one major safeguard that is missing from the Victorian legislation. Many people who support legalized "assisted dying" do so because they assume that it will only apply for patients with extreme, uncontrolled pain or other physical symptoms. But the legislation does not require that a patient has pain or any physical symptoms, only that they "be experiencing suffering that cannot be relieved in a manner that the person considers tolerable."[32] This suffering does not need to be physical, but includes suffering related to loss of autonomy or loss of dignity. And when we look at the reasons why patients access assisted dying in overseas jurisdictions where it is legal, pain is not the primary reason. In the US state of Oregon, where doctor-assisted suicide has been practiced for more than twenty years, less than a third of the patients who requested it had or were in fear of inadequate pain control. Instead, what motivated them were psychological factors: "depression, hopelessness, being tired of life, loss of control and loss of dignity."[33] Similarly, in the Netherlands, few patients receiving euthanasia had physical pain, but a majority were depressed. Yet in both Oregon and the Netherlands very few patients are referred to a psychiatrist. Ezekiel Emmanuel concludes, "Since psychological reasons dominate, one would think that requiring psychiatric evaluation would be a reasonable safeguard before providing euthanasia or physician-assisted suicide."[34]

But the Victorian legislation does not include this "reasonable safeguard," even when a doctor suspects depression, unless the person's decision-making capacity is in doubt, which would only occur in very severe mental illness. Indeed, the presence of mental illness in itself does not disqualify a person from accessing assisted dying.

31. *Voluntary Assisted Dying Act 2017* (Vic), sec. 9.
32. *Voluntary Assisted Dying Act 2017* (Vic), sec. 9.
33. Emanuel, "Euthanasia and Physician-Assisted Suicide," 339.
34. Emanuel, "Euthanasia and Physician-Assisted Suicide," 340.

There are two major problems with even the most stringent "safeguards" that might initially be put in place. The first is that the criteria for eligibility for "assisted dying" will inevitably be expanded, either in practice or by legislation. Overseas experience shows that initial safeguards become eroded in time. In the Netherlands and Belgium, patients with mental illness who are not terminally ill, people with dementia, and children are now among those euthanized. In the Netherlands, what began as a measure for exceptional cases has become so normalized that one in twenty-five deaths in the Netherlands is now the consequence of assisted dying.[35]

Therefore, although the criteria for eligibility for "assisted dying" in Victoria initially included only competent adults with a terminal illness, it will be (and already is) argued that these criteria are too restrictive.[36] Why should psychological suffering alone be excluded? Why should the patient have to be at the end of life, if they have a chronic debilitating condition which might last for years? And surely children can suffer as much as adults? And what about people with dementia? And so on.

Expansion of the criteria to include patients who are not terminally ill and non-competent patients is inevitable because of the logic of the two standard arguments for assisted dying, namely, the principles of respect of individual autonomy, and the obligation to relieve suffering. It is clear that each, if accepted as grounds for making an exception to the general wrongness of killing, would justify a much broader practice of "assisted dying" than is usually sought by its advocates. The two arguments are typically used together as a single justification, but they are logically separate. If the justification is respect for patient autonomy, then a request from a competent person is all that is required, and assisted dying cannot be limited to those who are "suffering" or who are terminally ill. And if the justification is the obligation to relieve suffering, it would apply equally to incompetent as to competent patients, and would justify assisted dying for children, dementia sufferers, and the intellectually impaired if it were judged that they were suffering.[37]

The second problem is the difficulty of monitoring and ensuring that safeguards are observed. As the report of the Victorian Parliament's *Inquiry into End of Life Choices* acknowledges, "Assisted dying occurs already in Victoria, despite being unlawful. It occurs within and outside of medical

---

35. Boer, "Following the Guide," 6.
36. Tomazin, "Assisted Dying Laws," paras. 8–13.
37. Callahan, "When Self-Determination Runs Amok," 54.

settings. The instances that occur within medicine are nearly impossible to police."[38] If some doctors are already prepared to break the law (and are able to get away with it) then there is no reason to believe that they will always comply with the legislated "safeguards." Monitoring relies on accurate reporting, and doctors may simply fail to report instances of assisted death which fail to meet the criteria. As Daniel Mulino notes, "Legalization simply shifts where hidden activities occur."[39] Even when doctors conscientiously seek to observe the criteria, it would be very difficult, if not impossible, to ascertain that a patient has not been subtly or not so subtly coerced into requesting "assisted dying." As previously noted, elderly, frail, and sick patients are especially vulnerable to suggestions that they are a burden and ought to request assisted dying.

But the argument, whether from principles or consequences, was lost in the Victorian Parliament, and we in Victoria now will need to learn how to live in a society where legal "assisted dying" is a reality. Within Christian communities, an alternative to both principles and consequences, virtue ethics, might be a more fruitful approach to living with this new reality. Virtue ethics focuses not so much on doing but on being, with priority given to character rather than right or wrong actions.

Whereas the premise of deontological theory is that "An action is right iff ["iff" means "if and only if"] it is in accordance with a moral rule or principle" and that of utilitarianism (a form of consequentialism) that "An action is right iff it promotes the best consequences" where "the best consequences are those in which happiness is maximized," the premise of virtue theory is that "An action is right iff it is what a virtuous agent would do in the circumstances." Further, "A virtuous agent is one who acts virtuously, that is, one who has and exercises the virtues," and "A virtue is a character trait a human being needs to flourish or live well."[40] There are as many virtue theories as there are notions of what it means to flourish or live well, and so the virtues particular to a tradition, whether it be the Aristotelian, Christian, or liberal individualist will not only be different, but will likely take different forms. As Hauerwas notes, "All virtue theories are not created equal."[41]

In Christian ethics it is recognized that the Scriptures are vitally concerned with the moral subject as well as the moral act. And there is no

---

38. Parliament of Victoria, *Inquiry into End of Life Choices*, 307.
39. Mulino, "Minority Report," 390.
40. Hursthouse, "Virtue Theory and Abortion," 223–46.
41. Hauerwas, "The Difference of Virtue," 249.

sharp distinction between a virtue and a deontological approach in the Christian tradition, since obedience to God's commands is a Christian virtue—though not the only one.[42] Flourishing or living well is living in accordance with our created human nature, which entails obeying God's commands. Richard Mouw expresses this in his defense of a divine command ethic (a form of deontology) which he says, along with virtue ethics, can be seen as "diverse proposed strategies for exhibiting a pattern of moral surrender to the divine will."[43]

No single ethical theory will account for the richness of the biblical material that may be brought to bear on the consideration of moral issues such as "assisted dying." Virtue ethics offers another perspective to complement the consideration of principles and consequences. It has a long history in Christian ethics, since Aquinas adapted the Aristotelian approach by adding the theological virtues of faith, hope, and love to the cardinal virtues of practical wisdom (prudence), courage, temperance, and justice. Yet there are numerous virtues commended in Scripture, including the fruit of the Spirit listed in Galatians 5:22–23. Unlike other virtue theories, Christian virtue ethics emphasizes that the development of the virtues in the believer is the work of God, and yet allows for human cooperation. It is God who is at work in us transforming us into the likeness of Christ (2 Cor 3:18; Rom 8:29).

Christian virtues are formed in a community of faith with a shared story. Such a community narrative is required to make sense of an individual's personal story. For Christian virtue ethicist Stanley Hauerwas, the most appropriate image for characterizing Scripture as a moral resource is that of a narrative. The biblical story provides the shared history and common set of interpretations that shape both the character of the Christian community and the individual believers who are a part of it.[44]

Concluding Remarks

Reflection on a number of Christian virtues would be relevant in considering the ethics of "assisted dying." For doctors, the virtue of humility: the recognition that medicine does not and should not have complete mastery over life and death, and that there are some kinds of suffering which

---

42. Hauerwas and Pinches, *Christians among the Virtues*, 138.
43. Mouw, *The God Who Commands*, 2.
44. Hauerwas, *Community of Character*, 58.

medicine cannot and should not seek to relieve. Theologian and bioethicist Paul Ramsey once rhetorically inquired whether "the purpose of modern medicine is to relieve the human condition of the human condition?" Not every human problem is susceptible to medical resolution, and to suppose that it is or ought to be reflects what the ancients called the vice of *hubris*, a pretension to unbridled control and unlimited knowledge.[45]

For relatives and friends of patients: compassion and kindness, expressed in ways that affirm their dignity and worth. And for patients: patience. Often conceived in passive terms, in the Christian tradition patience is much more positive: "Patience is the exercise of power" that involves the ability to continue "undisturbed by obstacles, delays or the temptation to quit."[46] It is based on confidence in the ultimate victory of good, the conclusion of salvation history that is yet to come, and can only be apprehended through faith and hope in the promises of God. The promise of the resurrection means that illness and death are not the end of the believer's story. The virtue of patience is also modeled on the patience of God, exemplified in the life of Christ, who bore the wrongs done to him without attempting to escape from them. Accordingly, suicide is out of the question.[47]

We need to form communities with an alternative narrative to the culture that enthrones individual choice as the ultimate value that trumps the common good, and that regards all suffering as meaningless and to be avoided at all costs. Communities that foster the virtues, especially humility, kindness, compassion and patience. Communities that embody in practical ways our affirmation that all human lives are valuable, including the disabled, the elderly, the sick, and the frail, so that no one is forced, because of pressure from their families, loneliness, and/or lack of availability of quality palliative care or mental health services to reach such a point of desperation and hopelessness that they feel they have "no choice" but to ask for assistance to end their lives.

Bibliography

American Medical Association. *Code of Medical Ethics* (2018). https://www.ama-assn.org/delivering-care/code-medical-ethics-caring-patients-end-life.

---

45. Campbell, "Religion and Moral Meaning," S8.
46. Callahan, "To Bear Wrongs Patiently," 274.
47. Hauerwas and Pinches, *Christians among the Virtues*, 173.

Ashby, Michael. "The Fallacies of Death Causation in Palliative Care." *Medical Journal of Australia* 166, no. 4 (1997) 176–77.

Australian Institute of Family Studies. *Elder Abuse.* https://aifs.gov.au/publications/elder-abuse/export.

Australian Medical Association. *Position Statement Euthanasia and Physician Assisted Suicide 2016.* https://ama.com.au/system/tdf/documents/AMA%20Position%20Statement%20on%20Euthanasia%20and%20Physician%20Assisted%20Suicide%202016.pdf?file=1&type=node&id=45402.

Beauchamp, Thomas, and James Childress. *Principles of Biomedical Ethics.* 4th ed. New York: Oxford University Press, 1994.

Boer, Theo A. "Following the Guide: Why Dutch and Belgian Experiences on Assisted Dying Should Concern Other Countries." *Zadok Perspectives* 131 (Winter, 2016) 5–8.

Boyle, Joseph. "Intentions, Christian Morality and Bioethics: Puzzles of Double Effect." *Christian Bioethics* 3, no. 2 (1997) 87–88.

Callahan, Daniel. "When Self-Determination Runs Amok." *The Hastings Center Report* 22, no. 2 (1992) 52–55.

Callahan, Sidney. "To Bear Wrongs Patiently." In *From Christ to the World*, edited by Wayne G. Boulton et al., 270–79. Grand Rapids: Eerdmans, 1998.

Campbell, Courtney S. "Religion and Moral Meaning in Bioethics." *The Hastings Center Report* 20, no. 4 (1990) S4–11.

Chustecka, Zosia. "Renowned Neurosurgeon on Assisted Dying and His 'Suicide Kit'" (April, 2017). https://www.medscape.com/viewarticle/879187.

Coleman, Diane. "Assisted Suicide and Disability: Another Perspective." Accessed January 19, 2019. https://dredf.org/public-policy/assisted-suicide/assisted-suicide-and-disability/.

Denton, Andrew. "An Argument for Assisted Dying in Australia" (November 2015). https://www.wheelercentre.com/notes/an-argument-for-assisted-dying-in-australia-andrew-denton-s-di-gribble-argument-in-full.

Emanuel, Ezekiel. "Euthanasia and Physician-Assisted Suicide: Focus on the Data." *Medical Journal of Australia* 206, no. 8 (May 2017) 339–40. https://www.mja.com.au/journal/2017/206/8/euthanasia-and-physician-assisted-suicide-focus-data.

Garcia, Elisa, and Henk Jochemsen. "Ethics of Stem Cell Research." In *Human Stem Cells: Source of Hope and Controversy*, edited by Henk Jochemsen, 63–125. Chicago: Bioethics, 2005.

Hauerwas, Stanley. *A Community of Character: Toward a Constructive Christian Social Ethic.* Notre Dame: University of Note Dame Press, 1981.

———. "The Difference of Virtue and the Difference It Makes: Courage Exemplified." *Modern Theology* 9 (July 1993) 249–64.

Hauerwas, Stanley, and Charles Pinches. *Christians among the Virtues: Theological Conversations with Ancient and Modern Ethics.* Notre Dame: University of Notre Dame Press, 1997.

Hill, Michael. *The How and Why of Love.* Kingsford, NSW: Matthias Media, 2002.

Hippocrates. "The Art." In *Hippocrates with an English Translation.* Translated and edited by W. H. S. Jones, 191–217. London and Cambridge, MA: Heinemann and Harvard University Press, 1977.

———. "The Oath." In *Hippocrates with an English Translation*. Translated and edited by W. H. S. Jones, 299–301. London and Cambridge, MA: Heinemann and Harvard University Press, 1977.

Hursthouse, Rosalind. "Virtue Theory and Abortion." *Philosophy and Public Affairs* 20, no. 3 (1991) 223–46.

Kelly, Joseph. "Andrew Denton Tells Church to Get Out of Euthanasia Debate." *The Australian* (August 2016). https://www.theaustralian.com.au/national-affairs/health/andrew-denton-tells-church-to-get-out-of-euthanasia-debate/news-story/79d96ef36771d7591fa850304b600966.

MacIntyre, Alasdair. *After Virtue*. Notre Dame: University of Notre Dame Press, 1984.

Menzies, Gordon. "Do Ends Justify the Means? Australia's Unprincipled Refugee Policy." *ABC Religion and Ethics* (4 November 2015). http://www.abc.net.au/religion/articles/2016/08/18/4522343.htm.

Mulino, Daniel. "Minority Report." In *Inquiry into End of Life Choices: Final Report*. Parliament of Victoria Legislative Council Legal and Social Issues Committee, 349–405 (June 2016). https://www.parliament.vic.gov.au/file_uploads/LSIC_pF3XBb2L.pdf.

Mouw, Richard. *The God Who Commands*. Notre Dame: University of Notre Dame Press, 1990.

Nelson, Mark T. "Consequentialism." In *New Dictionary of Christian Ethics and Pastoral Theology*, edited by D. J. Atkinson and D. H. Fields, 253–54. Leicester: IVP, 1995.

Oderberg, David. "Voluntary Euthanasia and Justice." In *Human Lives: Critical Essays on Consequentialist Bioethics*, edited by D. Oderberg and J. Laing, 225–40. London: MacMillan, 1997.

Parliament of Victoria Legislative Council Legal and Social Issues Committee. *Inquiry into End of Life Choices: Final Report* (June 2016). https://www.parliament.vic.gov.au/file_uploads/LSIC_pF3XBb2L.pdf.

Rachels, James. "Active and Passive Euthanasia." *The New England Journal of Medicine* 292, no. 2 (1975) 78–80.

Rationalist Society. "Submission to Parliament of Victoria's Legal and Social Issues Committee on End of Life Choices." https://www.rationalist.com.au/end-of-life-choices.

Somerville, Margaret. "Respect for Human Life? The 'Life Concepts' Informing End-of-Life Decision-Making" (February 2014). http://www.abc.net.au/religion/articles/2014/02/15/3945451.htm.

Stauch, Marc. "Causal Authorship and the Equality Principle: A Defence of the Acts/Omissions Distinction in Euthanasia." *Journal of Medical Ethics* 26, no. 4 (2000) 237–41.

Sulmasy, Daniel. "Killing and Allowing to Die: Another Look." *Journal of Law, Medicine and Ethics* 26, no. 1 (1998) 55–64.

Tomazin, Farrah. "Assisted Dying Laws: Call for Dementia Sufferers to Be Included." *The Age* (May 2017). https://www.theage.com.au/national/victoria/assisted-dying-laws-call-for-dementia-sufferers-to-be-included-20170527-gwejcf.html.

Victoria State Government. *Victorian Suicide Prevention Framework 2016–2025*. https://www2.health.vic.gov.au/about/publications/policiesandguidelines/victorian-suicide-prevention-framework-2016-2025.

Voluntary Assisted Dying Act 2017 (Vic), section 9.

PART II: ENGAGING ETHICALLY WITH WIDER SOCIETY

Wall, Patrick. "The Generation of Yet Another Myth on the Use of Narcotics." *Pain* 73, no. 2 (1997) 121–22.

World Medical Association. *Resolution on Euthanasia*. October, 2002. https://www.wma.net/policies-post/wma-resolution-on-euthanasia/.

Yuill, Kevin. "We Cannot Have 'Zero Suicides' If We Allow Euthanasia." *The Telegraph* (January 20, 2015). https://www.telegraph.co.uk/news/uknews/assisted-dying/11357000/We-cannot-have-zero-suicides-if-we-allow-euthanasia.html.

8

The Virtue of Docility in Global Theological Conversation

Thomas Kimber[1]

Introduction

THE RECENT MOVIE "THREE Billboards Outside Ebbing, Missouri" is a raw and confronting film. At times, it is difficult to watch. The movie focuses on the story of one mother's desperate longing for justice after the brutal rape and murder of her daughter. Unsatisfied with the seeming unconcern of the local police, she takes matters into her own hands and seeks not only justice but revenge. While the mother's actions take center stage in the drama, the story draws in multiple themes of social injustices in our day: racial tensions, sexual orientations, abuse in the church, the handicapped and physically challenged, etc. As the story unfolds, we discover that this is a town ripped apart by anger, fear, and prejudice. Everyone, it seems, has a story. The hinge point of the movie comes in a simple line: "Anger begets anger." In one subtle scene after another, the movie suggests that there may be a better way to deal with all of these issues. Anger and revenge simply lead to

---

1. I am indebted to my former student and teaching assistant, Nathaniel Warne, for inspiring me to reflect on this topic. I am also indebted to my colleague, Michael Bräutigam, for his assistance in providing resources and endless conversations that have helped to refine my thoughts.

more anger and revenge. At some point, the abused become perpetrators themselves. And so the cycle continues. Columnist Janet Albrechtsen, writing in *The Australian*, highlights an irony of our times:

> So many people try to signal virtue these days by expressing hate and anger. Pick an issue . . . we no longer just disagree with those with a different view. More and more, the imperative . . . is to hate the other side for holding views that suggest they are repositories of evil. When being angry at something makes you feel virtuous, anger becomes the drug of choice. The result is an age of outrage where listening to those we disagree with has become obsolete.[2]

The Lost Art of Listening

In a speech titled, "The Dying Art of Disagreement," Bret Stephens, a writer for the *New York Times*, laments the toxic nature of discourse in our world today, where there is much shouting but very little listening,[3] and where disagreements are settled with violence, aggression, or the removal and dismissal of the offending person. In his words, "What makes our disagreements so toxic is that we refuse to make eye contact with our opponents, or try to see things as they might, or find some middle ground. Instead, we fight each other from the safe distance of our separate islands of ideology and identity and listen intently to echoes of ourselves."[4]

In his speech, Stephens returns to the history of true discourse and disagreement. He laments the loss of real conversation over deep issues about which you and I may agree or disagree. Fundamentally, these conversations are never based on *misunderstanding*, but on a perfect *comprehension* of your opponent's perspective. As Stephens notes, "You need to grant your adversary moral respect, give him the intellectual benefit of doubt, have sympathy for his motives and participate empathically with his line of reasoning. And you need to allow for the possibility that you might yet be persuaded of what he has to say."[5]

While we may rightly decry these acts in society, we must acknowledge similar versions of it in the church. In recent decades we have witnessed a

---

2. Albrechtsen, "Moral Vanity," 22.
3. Stephens, "Dying Art of Disagreement."
4. Stephens, "Dying Art of Disagreement."
5. Stephens, "Dying Art of Disagreement."

dramatic shift in the global center of the church. The majority of Christians (approximately 67 percent) now live outside the Western world, predominantly in Africa and Asia. More than forty years ago, African theologian John Mbiti called attention to the fact that while the church in Africa was growing, theological conversation was virtually all one-sided. As he notes,

> We have eaten theology with you; we have drunk theology with you; we have dreamed theology with you. But it has all been one-sided; it has all been, in a sense, your theology.... We know you theologically. But the question is, do you know us theologically? Would you like to know us theologically? Can you know us theologically? And how can there be true theological reciprocity and mutuality, if only one side knows the other fairly well, while the other side either does not know or does not want to know the first side?[6]

Sadly, the question Mbiti raised in a previous generation is still being asked. To what extent are we in the church listening to one another across the various barriers of our society? Or, as Tim Hartman observes, "The future of constructive theology lies not in North America, Europe, or among white peoples. Instead, the future of constructive Christian theology lies in collaborations across cultural, ethnic, economic, and gender barriers."[7] In the classical sense, true discourse and even disagreement should not necessarily lead to division but to virtue. It requires the ability to enter into another person's world, to hear their story, and to be able to accurately articulate that story in meaningful and accurate ways.

Towards a Rediscovery of Docility

In facing these challenges, I find wisdom in the writings of Thomas Aquinas and his brief mention of a virtue that is rarely talked about in our times: the virtue of docility. The chief mark of docility is the willingness and readiness to be taught by others. Docility seeks true knowledge and understanding, and is considered the foundation of all other virtues as well as the foundation of our development as rational beings. Aquinas applies the virtue to the old as well as the young, to both teacher and student. He suggests that the student must "carefully, frequently and reverently apply his mind to the teachings of the learned, neither neglecting them through laziness, nor

---

6. Mbiti, "Theological Impotence," 16–17.
7. Hartman, "Moving from Christendom."

despising them through pride."⁸ And, conversely, those who are learned and more mature should demonstrate this virtue toward others, since no person is self-sufficient. Indeed, like many of my teaching colleagues, I find that my students are some of my best teachers. It can easily be applied beyond the classroom to virtually every relationship, especially to the parent and child, since this is where learning and relating to others begins.

In reflecting on Aquinas, Michael Barber explores this virtue in a way that relates not only to my work as an educator, but has far-reaching implications for human development and application in virtually every strata of life and society. He suggests, "It would seem that one of the key tasks of moral education involves converting the child's originary docility into a lasting virtue."⁹ The virtue of docility is much more than mere intellectual and cognitive understanding; it requires the ability to demonstrate awareness of others' feelings, thoughts, and needs. Indeed, the docile person demonstrates a willingness to learn from others what they, in fact, are feeling, thinking and needing. And, knowing these things, it causes one to appropriately adjust oneself and one's response in consideration of the other person's thoughts, feelings, and needs. Docility would lead me to regard even the one who is different from me with a measure of respect, believing fully that there is something I can learn from every human being. This combination of respect for every person and a willingness to learn from their life and their perspective enables me to approach the different other from a posture of openness and receptivity.

In his writings on virtue, Jonathan Edwards suggests that our growth in virtue and living them out in everyday life is nothing less than our participation in the divine life.¹⁰ For Edwards this understanding and growth in virtue will result in a deepening of our love for our neighbor and our love for God. Fundamentally, for Edwards and others, virtue is synonymous with compassion—the ability to suffer with another person. This, of course, requires that we enter into their world, share their story, listen with an open heart, and respond with full understanding. Similarly, Oliver O'Donovan points out that virtue typically is formed in the context of suffering.¹¹ In suffering we experience not an extinguishing of our humanity but a deep longing for a good which is lacking. To suffer alongside another person

8. Aquinas, *Summa Theologica*, II.2, 48, 1.
9. Barber, "Docility, Virtue of Virtues," 121.
10. McClymond and McDermott, *Theology of Jonathan Edwards*, 528.
11. O'Donovan, *Finding and Seeking*, 91.

THE VIRTUE OF DOCILITY IN GLOBAL THEOLOGICAL CONVERSATION

we must not only feel with them but we must long with them for the good which is lacking and which will ease their suffering.

It is no surprise to any of us that we are living in a world of increasing polarization on a variety of topics. Yet, the challenge before us must be seen not as a threat but an opportunity. In the light of this, what is our responsibility both in society and in the church to teach in such a way that we are forming in ourselves and in others the deeper virtues of a Christlike life?

Docility in Action

My thoughts turn to a couple of passages of Scripture. First, the reminder that Paul gives us in 1 Cor 8:1 that "knowledge puffs up." Who of us has not experienced that? In our places of learning and understanding, every one of us needs to be aware of the tendency to grow in arrogance and to think that our way is right and our knowledge is correct. It is a safeguard for all of us to keep in mind that as we continue to learn, we need to consciously strive for humility toward others with an attitude of openness and receptivity. The posture of being willing to learn is essential in us. Second, I love the picture of Jesus in Matt 18:3–4. In response to the question, "Who is greatest in the kingdom of heaven?," Jesus replies, "Truly, I say to you, unless you turn and become like little children, you will never enter the kingdom of heaven. Whoever humbles himself like this child is the greatest in the kingdom of heaven." I think there is much more to these verses than conversion. Jesus is teaching us about greatness in his kingdom—not just how to enter the kingdom, but how to live and grow and mature in his kingdom. It makes me wonder, in the light of my reflections on virtue, what does a young child have to teach us older, more mature men and women about what it means to be great in God's kingdom? Barber suggests that docility is the natural disposition of a child.[12] So how do we continue to nurture that in ourselves and in those whom we are training? What does Jesus's lesson about children teach us about the way to encourage virtue in ourselves and others? I think there are two important lessons.

First, it is important to understand the place of the child in Jewish society. Here is a person—and yes, a child *is* a person—who has virtually no importance in society. They are not to be taken seriously, and certainly not to be looked up to and admired. Yet Jesus places this child in front of these disciples and calls him or her "the greatest in God's kingdom." In this, Jesus

---

12. Barber, "Docility, Virtue of Virtues," 121.

is teaching us something very important about children in Jewish society. It indicates a sense of respect for even those whom society would consider the least. It bestows a humanness on those whom society would consider less than human. It teaches us about our own attitudes toward those who are not only different from ourselves, but whom we would consider less than ourselves. In God's eyes, they may be greater. And secondly, children teach us something about what it means to continue to grow in virtue in God's kingdom. There is a natural inquisitiveness, a disposition toward acceptance and simplicity in children that is winsome and attractive. But, as Barber would remind us, there is an original docility—a willingness to be taught and a desire to continue to learn. In considering these thoughts, I want to note four areas of implication for those who influence others in the church and in society.

First, in education and classroom teaching. Transformational teaching must go far beyond facts and information. Edmund Pincoffs suggests that in education we must not so much train people to make decisions but focus on excellence of character.[13] Emphasizing the virtue of docility and the host of other virtues that naturally flow from it, including honesty, compassion, and justice, will nurture a common quest for truth in community. These thoughts have already begun to spawn ideas about how to bring a deeper awareness of virtue and training for virtue in my classroom teaching. Certain forms of discussion, debate, and classroom interaction can foster the skills and attitudes needed to enter the world of another person for the purpose of deeper understanding and engagement with their ideas and thoughts. How often do we actually listen to the full argument a person is presenting before we form an opinion? Docility leads us to listen deeply and fully before we construct a rebuttal. It leads us to ask questions before we make statements. Yet, in our world this kind of response is becoming increasingly rare.

Second, in pastoral theology. The essence of compassion is to "feel with" another person. Yet, as pastors we are often trained to have the answers for whatever situation might come up. Understanding a theology of virtue helps us to take seriously the encounters and experiences of everyday life and to enter into the suffering of others. It helps us to find the connection between pastoral theology and spiritual theology—framing much of my responsibility as a pastor within the incarnational example of Jesus who entered our

---

13. Edmund L. Pincoffs, quoted in Michael Barber, "Docility, Virtue of Virtues," 120–21.

world and experienced fully our brokenness and took on our shame, yet with an ultimate view toward redemption and fulfilled hope.

Third, in global theological conversation. Over the past century we have seen a major shift in the global church. Whereas in the early 1900s the slogan of mission was "From the West to the rest," now the perspective is "From everywhere to everywhere." The church in the majority world is growing and maturing while the church in the West is in decline. Yet, to what extent are we listening to one another across the boundaries of our societies? How are we as missionaries and theologians doing at listening to and learning from the majority world church? Do we still view ourselves as the experts from the outside coming in with the answers, or can we learn to approach our brothers and sisters from other cultures with an attitude of openness and the question, "What can I learn from them?"

David Bosch observes that every one of us is "inclined to incarcerate the gospel within the narrow confines of his or her own predilections . . . We are irresistibly pulled towards onesidedness and reductionism."[14] We often hear in the Bible what we want it to say. And so, we must combine our listening to the Bible and the Spirit with listening to one another. This, of course, requires true humility and the laying aside of sectarian labels. In our humility, we must admit that none of us is self-sufficient and that we need the wisdom and experience of the global body of Christ. Indeed, as Jesus said, it is in our humility and ability to listen to and love one another that the genuineness of our faith would be proved and observed.

Fourth, we must understand our calling and our role as influencers in society. Those of us who work in theological higher education often think about the needs of the church and how we can train and influence a new generation of pastors and church leaders. But what is our responsibility to the larger society of which we are a part? We should consider Jeremiah's words to his people in exile: "Seek the welfare of the city where I have sent you into exile, and pray to the Lord on its behalf, for in its welfare you will find your welfare" (Jer 29:7). Too often, we have shirked our responsibility to influence our society in ways that contribute to the general good of all people. O'Donovan suggests that good exists in the world as an expression of God's own goodness.[15] Growth in virtue is not merely the application of a new set of actions, it is a new way of *being*. In other words, habituated virtue is incarnational. I believe that theologians, ministers, and students of

---

14. Bosch, "Emerging Paradigm for Mission," 504.
15. O'Donovan, *Finding and Seeking*, 71–72.

the Bible—and thus, virtually every believer—has the opportunity and the responsibility to enter more fully into the suffering of others as an expression of Jesus's own incarnation. We must consider the impact on society not merely through our words and opinions, but in our example of humble listening, compassionate caring, and our refusal to resort to names and labels in our desire to express the loving grace of Jesus.

The virtue of docility has the power to turn adversaries and enemies into advocates for one another who join together in seeking truth. Rather than defending ideologies, docile men and women recognize the mystery of learning, discover the emotion of suffering with and responding to others, and humbly admit the limits of human understanding. Can you imagine a world where people listen more than they speak? Where we desire to know others more than make ourselves known? Where we value the different other as a fellow human created in the image of God.

Bibliography

Albrechtsen, Janet. "The Moral Vanity of a Virtue-Signaller." In *The Weekend Australian* (January 27–28, 2018).

Aquinas, Thomas. *Summa Theologica*. Translated by the Fathers of the English Dominican Province. Westminster: Christian Classics, 1981.

Barber, Michael. "Docility, Virtue of Virtues: Lévinas and Virtue-Ethics." *International Philosophical Quarterly* 38, no. 2 (June 1998) 119–26.

Bosch, David. "An Emerging Paradigm for Mission." *Missiology: An International Review* 11, no. 4 (October 1983) 504.

McClymond Michael J., and Gerald. R. McDermott. *The Theology of Jonathan Edwards*. Oxford: Oxford University Press, 2012.

O'Donovan, Oliver. *Finding and Seeking: Ethics as Theology*. Vol. 2. Grand Rapids: Eerdmans, 2014.

Hartman, Tim. "Moving from Christendom to a Global Church." In *@ This Point: Theological Investigation in Church and Culture* 11, no. 1 (Spring 2016). Decatur, GA: Columbia Theological Seminary. http://www.atthispoint.net/editor-notes/moving-from-christendom-to-a-global-church/278.

Mbiti, John. "Theological Impotence and the Universality of the Church." In *Mission Trends No. 3: Third World Theologies*, edited by Gerald Anderson and Thomas Stransky. Grand Rapids: Eerdmans, 1976.

Stephens, Bret. "The Dying Art of Disagreement." *The 2017 Lowy Institute Media Award* (September 23, 2017). https://www.lowyinstitute.org/publications/dying-art-disagreement.

www.ingramcontent.com/pod-product-compliance
Lightning Source LLC
Chambersburg PA
CBHW051105160426
43193CB00010B/1320